WOMEN ON THE LAND

THE HIDDEN HEART OF RURAL AUSTRALIA

Margaret Alston

UNSW PRESS

Author's note

In order to protect the identities of the women
involved in this study, names and personal details
have been changed; essential details have not.

Published by
UNSW PRESS
Kensington NSW Australia 2052
Telephone (02) 398 8900
Fax (02) 398 3408

© Margaret Alston 1995
First published 1995

National Library of Australia
Cataloguing-in-Publication entry:

Women on the land: the hidden heart of rural Australia
  Bibliography.
  Includes index.
  ISBN 0 86840 382 2.

1. Rural women – Australia – Social conditions.
2. Farmer's spouses – Australia – Social conditions.
3. Women in Agriculture – Australia. I. Title.

305.40994

Text formatted in 11/12.5pt Berkeley
Printed by Southwood Press, Marrickville, NSW

Available in North America through:
ISBS Inc
Portland Oregon 97213-3644
Tel: (503) 287 3093
Fax: (503) 280 8832

Available in Singapore, Malaysia & Brunei through:
Publishers Marketing Services
Singapore 1232
Tel: (65) 256 516
Fax: (65) 253 0008

Science Team 2012.

SHORT LOAN

SEVEN DAY LOAN

This book is to be returned on
or before the date stamped below

Dedication

This book is dedicated, firstly, to the farm women who allowed me into their homes and their lives. Their trust and confidence in sharing intimate details with me has provided me with the motivation to complete this sometimes daunting task. As well, I would like especially to dedicate the book to a remarkable farmer who was one of the subjects of this research. Her wonderful spirit, her lifetime of hard work and her total commitment to her family and their farming life typify the unacknowledged efforts of farm women in this country. For more than 50 years, this woman laboured on her family farm, rearing five children and accomplishing with apparent ease the many tasks expected of a farm woman. Twenty-five years ago, she was widowed. She continued to run her farm right up to her death, at the age of 75 on 21 November 1992 after a short illness. Vale Bridget Moloney, your efforts are remembered and honoured in this work.

CONTENTS

CHAPTER 1

FARM WOMEN: WHO ARE THEY?

[Farm women are] a tremendous, unseen, unrecognisable force. They contribute a tremendous amount to the wealth, the stability and economic success of the farm. Added to that they contribute a tremendous amount to the community, to their schools and [they contribute] their organisational skills. And I think mostly it is unrecognised.

Farm woman, southern NSW, aged 42.

Dramatic changes have occurred in the nature of agricultural production in Australia this century. Until the mid-1950s, agriculture contributed 85 to 95 per cent of our export earnings. By the 1990s, this had dwindled to 30 to 35 per cent. Matching this staggering decline, there has been a reduction in the number of people living and working on farms. In 1953, 204,350 farms were listed in the census. Since then, nearly 80,000 have disappeared, and there are now only 125,615 farms remaining in production.[1] Many farming families have left the industry, and the rural workforce has declined by 100,000.[2]

Despite the rapid social changes taking place in the once-dominant agricultural industry, we know very little about the effects of such upheaval on the people most affected. What we do know is that the predominant type of farm-production unit is the farming family, with more than 90 per cent of farms being run by families and less than 7 per cent being run as corporate ventures.[3] It would not be too imprudent to suggest that almost all family farm arrangements include a husband and wife, and often, two or three generations. Therefore, by a process of deduction, we can conclude that there must be at least 250,000 farm women in this country. In fact, Kerry James, writing in 1989, suggests that there could be as many as 1.25 million women living and working on Australian farms.[4] Because the census does not accurately record the number of women who reside on farms, informed speculation is our best 'guesstimate'. Despite their large numbers, little is recorded about these women because they have rarely been the subjects of independent study and they live isolated from scrutiny.

Women have always had an integral role in agricultural production. In the less developed countries of Africa, women are largely responsible for agricultural production, while in more industrialised countries, they are involved in production in a less obvious way. Yet, there has been an international lack of acknowledgment of women's contributions to agriculture. Farming is presented as a male occupation, and women, when they are given any recognition at all, are depicted as 'helpers', wives, mothers or daughters of the principal operator. Few women feature in books on Australian agricultural history, but this is not because they have made little contribution to their industry. While Elizabeth Macarthur's name is well known in Australian folklore, less well known is Eliza Forlonge, a Scotswoman who walked more than 2400 kilometres through Saxony and Prussia in 1826, collecting the finest examples of Saxon sheep. She gathered and herded 100 of them to Hamburg, where they were shipped to Hull. From there, Eliza and her two sons walked them to Scotland for shipment to Australia. She repeated this remarkable journey three times. These sheep formed the basis of the superfine-wool industry in Australia, and in 1908, the Melbourne *Age* described Eliza Forlonge as someone who had 'notably stimulated and largely helped to mould the prosperity of an entire State and her name deserved to live for all time in our history.'[5] It is a cruel irony that we have all but forgotten Eliza and that her contributions to the wool industry are not as well known as John Macarthur's.

The devaluing of women and their contributions to agriculture has been a constant feature of our history. The process of writing women out of our agricultural records has been sanctioned at the highest levels. For example, official neglect appears to date from the late nineteenth century, when there was a sense of shame for a developing nation such as Australia to have to admit the extent of women's involvement in agriculture. In fact, in 1893, it was officially decided that women's farmwork would no longer be recorded.[6] As a result, censuses would no longer register farm wives as 'engaged in agricultural pursuits because that would create the impression elsewhere that women were in the habit of working in the fields as they are in some of the older countries of the world, but certainly not in Australia'.[7] While this decision did little to actually stop women working in agriculture, it did ensure that adequate records were not kept, and we have little officially recorded evidence of women working in agriculture. However, when other historical records such as newspapers, diaries and letters are examined, it becomes apparent that official data are not supported by first-hand accounts. Old copies of the *Argus* and the *Countryman* depict the difficult and hard life experienced by women earlier this century. Marilyn Lake reports on a letter submitted to the *Countryman* on 10 September 1926 by 'Una', who wrote:

> [The men's] hours on the machine may be long and laborious, but not so long as those of the woman who has to attend them. After the men's last meal for the day is over they can lie down and rest, or have a smoke, but not the women.
> ... If a farm won't pay without women having to make slaves of themselves in this fashion, well the quicker we give them up the better ...[8]

Other evidence of women's long and difficult hours on farms is not hard to find. Yet, at the time 'Una' and many others were writing their letters, few farm women were officially recorded as working in the agricultural industry.

Twentieth-century economic history has built on nineteenth-century bias against women. In seeking information on women's labour on farms from current census material, it became clear that women's history is still not being recorded by official means. Despite the fact that it is now acknowledged that farming is a joint venture requiring all members of the family to be involved,[9] censuses remain unreliable indicators of women's contributions. Men are recorded as farmers, but far fewer women are. For instance, in the 1991 Australian census data, approximately twice as many men as women are recorded as engaged in agricultural industry in most local government areas examined. Yet, from the evidence gained in researching this book, it appears that women's work is being discounted and devalued, and certainly not recorded. Economic historians still appear to see men as the norm and women as the 'other'. As a consequence, it is not possible to discover the realities of women's lives on farms by official means.

This book attempts to redress women's exclusion from the history of agriculture in Australia. Its purpose is to 'count women back in'. I carried out extensive research in farming areas in southern New South Wales during 1991; I interviewed 64 farm women at length. They were asked to speak about their lives and work, and a picture very different from the official version emerged from this research. The women I interviewed ranged in age from early twenties to late seventies, and so it was possible to gain not only a current perspective on women's role in agriculture, but also to examine their past contributions. The women were from two distinctly different geographical areas: one area, based on a large regional city, included a predominance of mixed livestock and cropping farms; the other area was in the more isolated broadacre cropping belt. Thus, it was possible to compare women from different industries and from different regions. I live in a rural community and am a farm woman myself, so this work is also informed by participant observation and a sense of intimate understanding of the societal and industrial structures which bind and constrain.

STRUCTURE OF THE BOOK

This book is presented in 11 chapters. Chapter 2 presents a feminist theoretical framework with which to examine the lives of farm women. Chapter 3 examines the changing nature of women's work on farms over the last two generations in the light of the changing circumstances in agriculture. Chapter 4 addresses the issue of farm women and their interaction with their families. Because farm families are so much more than kinship groupings, this chapter will look at the consequences for women living in a family which also operates as a production unit and which may include members of their husband's extended family. In Chapter 5 the issue of power is examined to determine the level of autonomy and control farm women have within their industry and within their own lives. Chapters 6, 7 and 8 examine the many aspects of women's work and the consequent economic contributions they make to their family enterprises. Their work in the home, on the farm, off the farm and in the community will be analysed. Chapter 9 deals with the effects of the economic crisis on farm families, in general, and farm women, in particular. Chapter 10 examines the issue of women's perceptions about themselves and their sense of their own place in agriculture. Finally, Chapter 11 summarises the position of farm women and examines the prospects for their future in the light of the developments in agriculture. The way women live and work on Australian farms, and the effects of changing economic circumstances on their lives, are the subject of this book.

FARM WOMEN AND WORK

I n examining the work of women, it becomes clear that established definitions of 'work' are biased against women. The definition of some types of effort as 'work' simply because they are remunerated, and other types of effort as not 'work' because they are not renumerated, disadvantages all women. In the farm sector, the narrow, business-oriented focus given to agricultural production in post-industrial capitalism has accorded recognition only to tasks directly related to production. Women's efforts, which are equally vital to production but which are less visible, are not recognised. For example, while men more often plant the crops, it is women who more often go to town for spare parts, help shift machinery and organise the meals around production. While such tasks are necessary to smooth production, they are not seen as contributing directly and have not been recognised as legitimate 'work'.

As well, the work of women in general and farm women in particular is structured by their responsibility for unpaid family work. Despite the continuing debate about the need for families to share domestic and family tasks, they are still viewed primarily as women's responsibility. Michael Bittman's study reveals that Australian women are doing 70 per cent of all domestic work in this country.[10] During the course of this research of Australian farm women I found them to be almost totally responsible for such work in more than 90 per cent of cases.[11] Such figures demonstrate that gender stereotyping is a continuing factor in Australia and that there has been no major shift in households to redress the imbalance.

A powerful disincentive for any such move for change is provided by the general acceptance of an ideology of domesticity for women. Along with the development of capitalism, there occurred a parallel development in the middle-class way of life. Middle-class values supported the ideology of women remaining in the home while men 'worked'. Women's position was, in fact, seen as essential to a Christian way of life. 'Domesticity was equated with morality'.[12] Perhaps not coincidentally, women's position in the home supported the process of capitalism and ensured male domination, as well as guaranteeing a reserve labour force ready to be tapped or neglected as circumstances dictate.

Despite its pervasiveness, the ideology of domesticity does little except sanction the assignment of domestic responsibility to women. Women are not confined to the home, they are merely constrained by such an ideology. When they work, they are forced to take on a double shift, such that everything they do is added to their responsibilities in the home. For many farm women, this means they may find themselves performing a triple shift as they balance domestic tasks, farmwork and off-farm work.

Constrained as they are by society's expectations, women are, nevertheless, moving into paid labour at an ever-increasing rate. Between 1966 and 1992, the Australian Bureau of Statistics (ABS) recorded that the labour force participation of married women increased from 29 per cent to 53 per cent, while the participation rate for non-married women remained stable at about 50 per cent.[13] Farm women, like their urban counterparts, are joining the paid labour force when work is available. Fifty per cent of the farm women in this study are in paid work, although their work is characterised by low pay, poor conditions and insecurity. Furthermore, 32 per cent of the farm women working off the farm report being overqualified for their positions. Despite their movement into the paid labour market, farm women have to juggle vastly different expectations because their work is shaped by tradition. Being a 'farm wife' is a unique occupation given legitimacy in rural society, despite the fact that there is no equivalent 'farm husband' role.[14] It is depicted as a biologically determined productive and reproductive role which includes taking full responsibility for unpaid family work, taking on an organising role in the enterprise and performing an expressive role in conflict negotiation and mediation between husband and son/s.[15] In fact, Boulding describes farm women's work as 'the glue that holds the farm together'.[16] For those who choose to move off the farm to work, they add to their ill-defined work as a 'farm wife'. Yet, their off-farm income is often vital to the survival of the enterprise. As well, women are contributing a great deal of voluntary labour to their communities and are following the worldwide trend to replace hired labour on their farms.

WOMEN'S PLACE IN FARM FAMILIES

W omen are often seen as secondary in their relationships on the farm. One of the most striking elements of family farming is the practice of passing the farm from father to son (patrilineal inheritance), a practice which ensures that farms are owned and controlled by men and that women's most common point of entry to farming is through marriage. Women are often in a subordinate relationship with members of their husband's extended family, and may have to seek permission from their extended family to purchase goods for consumption. Shirley Gould reports the case of Lucy, a farm woman in northern New South Wales, who said:

Right now, our bedroom needs curtains, and before I can buy the material, the men [husband, father-in-law and two brothers-in-law] discuss it at a meeting. They decide which daughter-in-law can have the money for curtains or some other thing for their house. We don't even go to the meeting. We wait at home like children waiting for Santa Claus.[17]

It is not uncommon for the yearly farm income allocations to be decided in meetings from which women are excluded.[18] Political economists who argue that the farm family labour unit is an example of interdependence between men and women choose to overlook the fact that it be the site of exploitation of women and children who live and work within a gendered hierarchical system.

The gendered nature of farming is supported and fostered by all forms of rural media. Agricultural commercials are more often than not directed to the 'man on the land'. A very successful beef commercial in recent years was directed at women, exhorting them to 'feed the man meat'. Men control the agenda in rural industries and rural political bodies, and in rural communities they dominate most of the public space. Men's activities and sports are accorded greater legitimacy, while women facilitate them by catering, washing clothes and serving food.[19] The options for women are greatly reduced in rural areas and women moving into rural communities report finding their circumstances stifling.[20] A woman marrying into a farm family must face being seen by the community as secondary ('the missus') and subordinate to any family business arrangement, and possibly even a threat to the stability of the legal arrangement. She may never be taken into the legal partnership because of the concern that she may divorce the son and take half the farm. For women raised in urban areas, many of whom are accustomed to having their own independent income and a strong sense of self-worth, such a situation can be devastating.

THE FAMILY FARM

F amily farming has been the dominant mode of agricultural production in this country since the Selection Acts were enforced in the nineteenth century. Australian policy was influenced by the 'yeoman' ideal of English farming, which emphasised family production and self-sufficiency. It was essentially a pre-capitalist and pre-industrial form of organisation, pushed by the state as an acceptable form of capitalist development in a land which had a strong ideology of equal opportunity.

Advances in technology and the exigencies of a capitalist marketplace have seen rapid changes in the business of farming. Farms now operate in a world marketplace, such that a drought in the United States may be good news for Australian farmers, while overproduction in the US could spell disaster. Currently, underproduction of rice in Japan has provided a bonus for rice growers in the Murrumbidgee Irrigation Area of New South Wales. The fortunes of farming families are at the mercy of unpredictable events. The reliance on the fickleness of world markets has been a recent development in agriculture. Previous generations of farm families were able to predict their yearly, and even five-yearly, incomes with a great degree of certainty. This is no longer the case.

Another factor influencing the viability of farming families has been the encroachment of agribusiness control in agriculture. Agribusinesses are the large companies that serve the agricultural industry. Agribusinesses now control most of the inputs to agriculture and are increasingly controlling the outputs, with the result that farmers are paying higher input prices for such items as fertilisers and chemicals and are receiving less for their outputs. Agribusinesses control the price of food, and farmers are forced into a position where they are 'price takers' and not 'price makers'.[21] As a result of the increasing difficulties in agriculture, more families are leaving, and those remaining are increasing their level of indebtedness. The Australian Bureau of Agricultural and Resource Economics (ABARE) estimated that 25 per cent of broadacre farms had debts in excess of $128,600 in 1991/2 and that around 12 per cent had debts exceeding $353,100.[22]

A parallel development in agriculture is the increasing size of farms. Larger farms are taking over smaller ones, with the result that farms have become bigger, on average, over the last 50 years. While larger farms are able to survive more easily in the current economic circumstances, there does appear to be a trend developing towards larger production units at one end of the spectrum and smaller, poorer operations at the other. These smaller, more marginal family farms are holding on by adopting survival measures such as 'belt-tightening', whereby they reduce expenditure on agricultural inputs and reduce their purchases of consumables.[23] Inevitably, their standard of living slides into poverty.

One strategy adopted by some farmers to secure stable markets is the practice of contract farming. Entering into an arrangement with a processor to produce a certain type of product at a fixed price at least provides stability. However, for some, such as the peach growers of Leeton who contracted with the now-bankrupt Letona cannery, this has led to ruin. While this downturn is the result of government policies on imports and the volatility of the marketplace, many farmers are prepared to take such risks in the interest of protecting their incomes. Contract farming provides a level of security but it reduces the options for farmers who continue to bear the risks of failed crops, while losing much of their control over production. They may, in fact, end up as little more than risk-taking employees.

Many farmers are also diversifying their incomes by accessing off-farm sources of cash. While this may take the form of investments, it is more commonly the case that a family member will work off the farm. In my study, I discovered that 44 per cent of farm men are working, usually part-time, off their farms in such work as shearing, rouseabouting in woolsheds, wool classing or contracting work with their own machinery. Fifty per cent of farm women are also working off the farm in usually part-time work. Off-farm work is often the only secure source of income in the household.

The changes in agriculture have forced farm families to adopt various strategies to remain viable. Various options are pursued in this endeavour, which have resulted in the tightening of agribusiness control of production, an increase in the level of indebtedness, changes in the way technologies are incorporated into farming, an increase in the level of contract farming and the development of larger, more capital-intensive farms, at one end of the scale, and smaller farms reliant on off-farm income, at the other end. The work of individual farm women is very much structured by the effects of these developments on their own farms. On larger farms, they do very little physical labour and may work off the farm and in the community. On smaller farms, their work, both on the farm and off, may be crucial for the survival of their family in farming. The way individual farm women make sense of, and balance, their work roles will be discussed in later chapters. What is important to note here is that farm women structure their lives around circumstances which are beyond their control.

SUMMARY

W omen are invisible actors in agriculture, accorded little recognition. Yet this book reveals their enormous contributions to families, industry and communities. The work of women in general and farm women in particular has long been undervalued in this country. Census statistics and the restricted definition of 'work', ensure that the devastating underreporting of the efforts of women are officially sanctioned. Despite this, the agriculture industry, which is experiencing a prolonged period of instability, relies heavily on the input of women to survive. Women are working on farms, in paid work and in their communities to ensure that family farming remains the dominant mode of agricultural production.

A FEMINIST FOCUS ON THE LIVES OF FARM WOMEN

Well all I can say is it's a man's world and any woman who thinks it isn't is a pickled onion!
67-year-old farm woman, southern New South Wales.

T he women's movement and the consequent feminist analysis have led to the re-evaluation of women's working and family lives. This analysis forms part of the socially constructed consciousness of farming women and, as such, cannot be ignored. However, there is considerable evidence that the women's movement has had little effect on farm women, in Australia at least, and, in fact, agriculture has been described as the last remaining area of female conservatism.[1] Yet, when one looks at the lives of farm women, it appears that a lot of what farm women do would be viewed as 'men's work' in an urban context. This book will show that farm women are increasingly involved in such tasks as driving heavy machinery and tending livestock, and they are performing an integral role in their enterprise. As well, there are an increasing number of partnership arrangements (often, husband–wife partnerships) on family farms. Consequently, when one looks at the lives and work of farm women, it would at first appear that they have overcome many barriers still to be tackled by other women. Yet, evidence suggests that they retain their conservatism; to understand this phenomenon, a searching theoretical appraisal is needed.

Chapter 2
SOCIOLOGICAL THEORISING

W omen have been excluded from the mainstream of sociological theorising until very recently. For much of the twentieth century, such theorising was dominated by structural functionalism; in particular, that of Talcott Parsons. Parsons's sex-role theory detailed rigid role prescriptions for women which were seen to represent 'normal' behaviour.[2] These prescriptions systematically outlined how women *ought* to be, rather than how they *were*. There was a very clear purpose in such assigned roles, as they were seen as functional for the stability and proper functioning of society. Women were viewed as having an 'expressive', or social–emotional function, acting to ease the tension of adult males; these roles were seen as essential and were so rigidly prescribed that women who deviated from them were regarded as abnormal or even mad.[3] The ideology of sex roles, espoused by structural functionalists, and circulated by the media, was a major hegemonic element in the continued subordination of women for much of this century. These functionalist pronouncements had a profound influence on conservative women, who sought to follow the dictates society set out for them.

Assigning roles on the basis of biological sex led to the development of ideological stereotypes which dictated that men should 'work' and support their family, while women should be primarily responsible for housework and children and provide the emotional anchor in the home. A sharp demarcation between public and private spheres developed, with men being active participants in the 'more important' public sphere, while women became associated with the 'less important' private sphere.

The resurgence in popularity that Marxism enjoyed in academic circles from the late 1960s and 1970s resurrected the concepts of alienation, power, oppression and exploitation, concepts which should have illuminated the lives of women. However, Marx himself did not delve into women's unique problems, preferring to see men's and women's exploitation as having the same source.[4] Even the neo-Marxists, who have questioned certain of Marx's concepts, have failed to question the hierarchical sexual ordering of Western capitalist society. Thus, leftist women found themselves alienated from Marxism.

In addressing the invisibility of women in sociological theorising generally, A. March suggests that theorists of all persuasions espoused androcentrism by the devices of exclusion, pseudo-inclusion and alienation.[5] Exclusion occurred because much of the theorising concentrated on male-dominated institutions, or the 'public' sphere. Max Weber, for example, was guilty of focusing attention on social processes and activities in which women were only marginally involved. Pseudo-inclusion occurred when women were included but when their experiences were, nevertheless, marginalised. For example, although female statistics did not support Emile Durkheim's theory of suicide, he chose to treat women as a special case rather than change the theory. Alienation occurred when theories included women but continued to distort their lives or contributions — women's experience was dealt with through male categories. Marxist theories are guilty of this fault in that they locate women only in relation to a male and his connections to other men with respect to the means of production.

The lack of women-focused sociological research before the development of feminism, and the centrality of functionalism, meant that women's options were greatly reduced and their lives were rendered invisible. For example, Gretchen Poiner suggests that country women have been, at best, 'a shadowy presence' in the published literature.[6] Farm women have been particularly disadvantaged by this process and have been described as 'invisible farmers', resulting in their having been ignored by scholars and policy-makers until recently.[7]

FEMINIST THEORY

In response to the androcentric nature of social and political theorising and their alienation from Marxism, the second wave of feminism was developed by some women who sought to break away from the left. As Marxism regained popularity in the 1970s, women who supported the left found themselves marginalised, because their concerns were, at best, seen as peripheral. As Ann Curthoys explains, '… it was quite apparent that the Left had never considered women in a revolutionary perspective, expecting us to remain its faithful servants and supporters in the great struggle'.[8]

Although this second wave still draws heavily on Marxist concepts, it is the first truly woman-focused theory. Second-wave feminism draws much from the work of Simone de Beauvoir, who demonstrates that men view women as fundamentally different from themselves, and consequently, reduce them to a category of 'other'. De Beauvoir saw that women had not been seen as autonomous but were defined in male terms. Humanity itself was seen to be male, she argued, and so women were 'other'.[9] Initially, feminists strove to prove that men and women were, in fact, not fundamentally different from each other. However, latter-day feminists have moved away from this position to proclaim the virtues of difference.

Feminism is concerned with the premise that Western society is governed in all its spheres by patriarchal beliefs, attitudes and values, and in which women, as a group, are both undervalued and underrepresented. Feminism became the first theory to focus on the previously marginalised world of women. Consequently, feminism generally has been defined, at least by one writer, as 'an analysis of women's subordination for the purpose of figuring out how to change it'.[10] All schools of feminism agree on the central premise of women's subordination and oppression, and acknowledge gender as a major determinant of human relations.[11] The differing schools of feminism are all committed to seeking a better life for women and differ largely only in their approach to change. There are four distinct schools of feminist thought that have developed since the emergence of the second wave of feminism in the late sixties and early seventies, although these schools are becoming less well defined and more fluid as the century draws to a close. These schools are radical feminism; socialist feminism; reform, or liberal, feminism; and postmodern feminism. In Australia, the women's movement was begun by radical feminists who contributed most in terms of energy and theory.

SEX ROLES, IDEOLOGY AND PATRIARCHY

I n the early 1970s, radical feminists first turned their attention to an analysis of sex-role theory, which, as a result of Parsonian structural functionalism, sustained the superordinate role of men and the subordinate role of women. Because structural functionalism perceived these roles as being biologically determined, they were regarded as fixed and rigid. By contrast, Kate Millet, an American radical feminist, indicated the conceptual difference between sex and gender, and further demonstrated that male/female roles were, in fact, gender determined.[12]

The view that sex and gender were conceptually different rapidly gained widespread support among radical feminists and led to vigorous feminist theorising. Whereas sex was seen to be biologically determined, gender was regarded as a more insidious, 'culturally and socially shaped cluster of expectations, attributes, and behaviours assigned to that category of human being by the society into which the child was born'.[13] In other words, gender was viewed as representing the social behaviour that society expected, and which it identified with either the male sex or with the female sex. In this way, gender has come to be socially constructed as a division of labour which differentiates the roles adopted by men and by women, and as a result of this division of labour, there has been a fairly recent historical emergence of 'woman's place'.

Whereas the roles of mother, homemaker and wife are seen from an anti-feminist point of view to be biologically determined, no such biologically determined male role exists. For working mothers, this state of affairs has resulted in problems of identification. Whereas men are usually defined by their occupation and not as 'working fathers', women who work have difficulty integrating their work role with that of being a mother. Indeed, they are still defined in terms of their mothering role, irrespective of their work roles and irrespective of the fact that so many married women are gainfully employed. Farm women are often referred to in the literature, and identify themselves, as farm wives, whereas it is difficult to imagine men identifying themselves or others as farm husbands. Women's mothering and spousal roles have, generally, resulted in their relegation to the private, domestic sphere, which is legitimated by the prevailing patriarchal ideology that associates women with nature and men with culture. For farm women, this has led to an ideology of 'wifehood' which prescribes certain work as the province of women.[14]

The feminist analysis of ideology allows us to understand why the work of farm women is given so little public value despite their enormous contributions to farm family survival. Prevailing rural ideology is strongly conservative. The National Party, a political party originally established to look after the interests of farmers, has in the past supported capital punishment, opposed affirmative action and abortion, and, more recently, has floated the idea of conscription. The traditional conservatism of farm families is based on ideals which have included an acceptance of male hegemony; a belief in the domestic ideology for women; a firm support for the sexual division of labour; a commitment to self-sufficiency and rugged individualism; a belief in the inalienable human right and freedom to use the land as one sees fit; and a strong rejection of a welfare mentality. All these aspects of rural ideology have acted to reinforce and preserve family farming and family ownership of land in its present form. Under adverse conditions, farming families have drawn strength from the ideology, a factor which has made them highly resistant to change. The term 'country consciousness' has been used to describe the traditional style of farming family relationship in Australia.[15]

S. Stebbings drew attention to the 'country woman' mentality, whereby women themselves were said to hold traditional ideas.[16] It has been argued that women support the male-oriented ideology which deprives them of power and legitimates their subordination because of their socialisation and continuing false consciousness.[17] It could be argued that rather than having false consciousness, farm women are, in fact, prepared to collude in this public marginalisation in exchange for their significant private power and because of the power dynamics which operate to subordinate their concerns. However, their collusion, or compliance, needs to be understood in terms of the enormous constraints on women which may make it easier to collude than to attempt to change constraining structures such as the law, customs, economic pressure and educational practices. As well, the threat of social stigma for those who challenge the established order makes it difficult for women to act.[18]

Whatever the case, the results of sex-role stereotypes can be devastating. The consequences of women's invisibility in the literature have been inadequate agricultural analysis and discriminatory public policies. Federal and State agricultural programs in Australia and other Western countries such as the US have tended to exclude women because the labour of farm women is ignored and their role is seen as domestically centred.[19] An upshot of this view is that Western bias has been transferred to Third World countries by aid programs, so that agricultural training is being offered only to men, even though women do a large proportion of farming in subsistence economies.

There has been much useful feminist analysis of the ideological notion of the sexual division of labour that throws light on the restrictions on farm women. The allocation of the breadwinner role to the male and the childcare and housewife role to the female has been ideologically interpreted as biologically determined by women's reproductive function. However, the only truly biologically determined roles are childbearing and breastfeeding, while the rest are socially constructed gender divisions which have acted to reduce the options of women. The sexual division of labour has been aided by the greater advantages men enjoy in wages and workplace conditions and access to education and training, which result in families making a logical, as well as an ideological choice to allocate the domestic and childcaring tasks to women. There is, then, 'a material basis for the perpetuation of the sexual division of labour in the family and of the ideology of motherhood'.[20] This argument is used to justify the allocation of the major domestic responsibilities to farm women. In times of reasonable returns, men are usually able to earn more from farming than women can from off-farm work. Together with a lack of fulfilling off-farm employment in isolated areas, it becomes logical to expect women to take the responsibility for all domestic and childcare tasks. However, the current crisis in agriculture, which has seen women taking off-farm work, replacing hired labour on farms and continuing to take major responsibility for domestic work, has exposed the disadvantages such a system imposes on women.

The ideological notion of the sexual division of labour is not supported in reality, because despite the structural barriers, women are under increasing pressure to work on as well as off the farm. In fact, the evidence presented in this book supports the view put forward by some theorists that the work of farm women is maintaining the economic viability of the family farm.[21] As Curthoys suggests, what is needed is '... a vast ideological change among men, so that they are forced to abandon the ideology of sexism, and so that they cease to see child care (along with housework) as inevitably and biologically women's work'.[22]

A useful concept for understanding the invisibility of farm women in the literature, but one which has divided feminist theorists, is the idea of 'the system of patriarchy', a phrase coined by Millet to describe the way men exert control over women.[23] The term patriarchy gained credence among feminist theorists because they saw it as a useful concept for describing Betty Friedan's 'problem with no name'.[24] Patriarchy is defined as the system whereby men have more power and economic privilege than women for no reason other than their maleness. According to such theories, the male hierarchical ordering of society is preserved through the sexual division of labour in society. Radical feminists such as Millet see men as the oppressors of women because men embody the relations of patriarchy.

Although radical feminists and socialist feminists accept patriarchy as 'the norm',[25] socialist feminists have difficulty in dealing with the concept. Clare Burton argues there can be no specific definition of patriarchy, because it varies within social formations at particular points in history,[26] and Curthoys suggests that it is unworkable within socialist feminism, because it treats men and women as separate and opposing groups, disregarding other power relations and inequalities which cut across sexual lines.[27] This is a dilemma for socialist feminists who are committed to a class analysis by their combined Marxist–feminist approach, and who, by placing class foremost in their class–gender approach, have difficulty dealing with the hierarchical ordering of society based on gender.

Whatever one's views on the concept and its place in theorising, a feminist observer would note that farm women face the effects of patriarchy throughout their lives, and the most telling indicator of this is their lack of control over the resources of agriculture. Despite the increasing number of husband–wife partnerships on farms, it is worth noting that the numbers increased when it became advanta-

geous because of tax incentives and not because women were necessarily gaining more power (or more control over resources).[28]
Women are limited to entering agriculture through marriage. They
rarely figure in inheritance, which is the most usual way farms are
acquired, and are often, therefore, effectively disinherited if their
natal family is a farm family. As this book will reveal, a farm woman's position is marginal if her husband is involved in a partnership
with his parents, and even more marginal if he is involved with his
brothers. Further, treatment of farm women under family law has
often been discriminatory: and on divorce, their claims to their mat-
rimonial home have not been given the same recognition as the
claims of urban women[29] and nor has the amount of work they may
have done been considered in property settlements.[30] A major con-
sideration in the past has been to ensure the male farmer is left with
a viable production unit. Consequently, farm women escaping a vio-
lent or unfulfilling marriage have had difficulty achieving an equitable settlement, and because of the difficulty of splitting farm
assets, may be left destitute.[31]

THE PERSONAL IS POLITICAL

A major problem for conservative women, and arguably for
many farm women, being confronted by feminist ideology has been
the stridency with which such ideas as patriarchy and opposition
to men have been proclaimed by some feminists. The attacks on
personal relationships with men made by the early wave of feminists have been difficult for some women to understand, and so,
have alienated many. For example, 'the personal is the political'
became the catchcry of the second feminist wave. Given their
growing awareness of the unequal power relations that existed
between men and women, and their acknowledgment of the gender ordering of society, feminists generally came to believe that the
most intimate relationships between men and women contained a
political dimension.[32] Radical feminists and socialist feminists both
realised that, generally, feminist theory was embedded in a political
context and could not be separated from practice. 'Feminist theory,
irrespective of its internal divisions, was, then ... all about change,
and gave a political expression ... to the problem faced by women

in both their public and private lives.'[33] Whereas socialist feminists seem to have encountered difficulties with their class–gender perspective, radical feminists appear to have bridged the theoretical gap between the public and private spheres. Sex as personal was seen to be political, and so, women were seen to share their oppression as a sex class. The ordering of both society and of family relations were viewed as similar problems.

Early second-wave feminists concentrated on the distinction between sex and gender, and argued for a reduction in the polarisation of spheres and its replacement with some form of androgyny.[34] As a result of this early theorising, and because of selective reporting in the media, women were encouraged to enter public spheres without any attention being focused on the structures of patriarchy which oppressed women. It was seen as possible for women merely to adapt to the existing, patriachal structures. As a result of these developments, the focus of feminist theorising changed in the mid-seventies to stressing the differences between men and women. Instead of trying to minimise the differences between men and women, feminists looked at the elements of female experience which were 'potential sources of strength'.[35] While this trend in feminism has great potential to incorporate the concerns of conservative women, there has been a disturbing focus on the so-called 'moral superiority of women'.[36]

To date, feminism has had a limited but nevertheless an important effect on social structure. Women have been recruited into areas of public life from which they were previously excluded, such as in law, medicine and so on. However, basic structural changes called for by the early radical feminists have not occurred, and women now find their marginal gains under threat from the New Right.

One site of disagreement that farm women have with feminists is their view of the role of the state. Farm women, as part of the farm family unit, have always viewed the state with suspicion. The state has maintained a heavy involvement in Australian agriculture since first settlement in 1788, and farming families have often viewed the state as acting contrary to their interests. (For instance, the action of the then federal Minister for Agriculture, John Kerin, to lower the floor price for wool in 1991 was a glaring example of state intervention against the perceived interests of farmers.) It is important to note this fact, because feminists sometimes find themselves in a dilemma concerning state intervention. On the one hand, they seek recourse to the state to achieve autonomy, while on the other hand they know that increased state control limits autonomy. By contrast, while farm women are aware of the necessity for the state's statutory marketing bodies, they see the state acting to obstruct the farming unit, and it is the farming unit with which they identify. Because of this identification, measures of individual autonomy, achievable only by recourse to the state, are thus subsumed and, in fact, farm women report feeling guilty when they seek services such as childcare for themselves.

THE FAMILY

M any conservative women have been alienated by the pronouncements of some feminists on the subject of the family which have been highlighted by the media. In general, feminists have been very critical of the nuclear family.[37] Radical feminists, in particular, consider that the first and greatest oppression was, and is, of women by men, and that the embodiment of this oppression is the nuclear family, where, according to the radical feminist Firestone, an inherently unequal power distribution based on biology exists.[38] The reproductive capacity of women is regarded as central to their subordinate position. For Firestone, the solution lies in the dissolution of the biological family and its replacement with artificial reproduction, and the replacement of privatised childcare with socialised childcare. However, I feel that Firestone's solution represents a position reached by some feminists who see freedom negatively. Therefore, her position is unacceptable because it does not provide a model of positive integration of mind and body for women. In finding that sexuality is the cause of women's oppression, Firestone seeks to overcome this by taking the sexual manifestations away from women. In so doing, she imposes a cultural assessment of women's biology as unequal and fails to reassess the cultural prescription.

Socialist feminists, generally, disagree with Firestone's views.[39] They claim that women's oppression lies not only with biological reproduction, but also with women's position in economic reproduction, with the regulation and control of sexuality and with the socialisation of children. What feminist theorists do agree on is the relation of women's oppression to the ideological relegation of women to the private sphere. In fact, Elizabeth Janeway argues that women's relegation to the private, domestic sphere of the home was the assumption underlying the ideology that rendered women relatively powerless.[40] Despite much evidence to the contrary, women are still viewed as essentially associated with the private sphere. Biological determinism, which underlies this ideological assumption, is a convenient argument that has allowed women to be oppressed both in the private sphere and in the public sphere when they venture out to work. Ideologically viewed as mothers or potential mothers, their work is devalued, the labour market is allowed to remain segregated and women's wages are, on average, far less than men's.

Feminists believe the family supports and preserves the patriarchal system. 'Patriarchy's chief institution is the family'.[41] Some argue that in order for the hierarchical sexual division of society to be changed, the biological family must be examined. The assumption of biological determinism, upon which the sexual division of labour rests, needs to be challenged and understood as merely a gender ordering of roles. As we have seen, biological determinism is an immutable concept which gives validity to women's powerlessness, whereas gender stereotyping is not immutable and allows women their revolutionary potential or 'species being', because women are free to escape from and change such stereotyping.[42]

The stereotypical position of women in the family has been useful for the ideological notion of the family as a haven and emotional refuge, because it has been women who have been expected to provide this refuge as part of their 'emotive' role.[43] While, historically, the family has become more isolated, so, too, have women become more isolated within the private sphere, with the result that the social reproduction of gender and sexual inequality are rigidly perpetuated. Production and reproduction became separated in urban areas as capitalism developed, resulting in women's reproductive role being seen as non-productive.

As a consequence of this development, women in the labour force are forced to bear the burden of the double day, because their domestic work is not defined as 'work' at all. Childcare is, likewise, seen as unimportant and insignificant to production, and so is not worthy of tax concessions, despite the enormous difficulties women in general, and farm women in particular, who work outside the home have juggling work commitments with childcare.

The radical feminists' assessment of this role the family takes in supporting patriarchy has all too often led them to advocate the abandonment of the family altogether. However, this call has made the feminist movement very vulnerable to attack from conservatives, including many women and, arguably, many farm women. I do not support such a call. Rather, abandonment of gender stereotyping and a restructuring of the hierarchical, patriarchal structure of the family should be the focus of feminist theorising. Because of feminist theory's urban focus, it has developed around the notion of separate spheres for workplace and home. However, the farm family, with its precapitalist mode of production, has no such dichotomy between work and home. In fact, it could be argued that because of the unique relationship between farm women and their families, feminism's call to expose the oppression of the family, and perhaps to abandon it, has alienated such women because of its lack of relevance to their lives.

Farm women are part of an economic unit, the farm family, which provides occupational identity and opportunity for personal fulfilment. Hostility towards men is unacceptable in a system that depends on a high degree of cooperation. The integration of the farm and the home makes it difficult to apply urbanised theoretical models, because the more farm women become involved in the productive side of the enterprise, the more they are enmeshed in family relationships. Despite the acceptance by farm women of the philosophy of separate spheres, there is, in fact, very little separation between work and home. For urban women, on the other hand, their work frees them from the constraints of kinship and allows them a measure of personal autonomy, although they may only be 'free' to seek exploitation in the workforce. For farm women, their interdependency with

farm men, essential to successful family farming, does not necessarily translate into equality. Nevertheless, the appeal of the family farm way of life is arguably stronger than that of the family per
se, because it appears to be not only an emotional sanctuary but
also an escape from the capitalist mode of production. This, of
course, is not entirely correct, because farms are now dependent
on world markets and agribusiness corporations. However, wom-
en's family consciousness, which results from their involvement
in the family farm unit and the patrilineal system of farm inheritance leads farm women to be threatened by any attack on the
family, despite the fact that farm family arrangements place
restrictions on the autonomy of farm women. Feminist theorists
have failed to note their urban bias and have not given recognition to the concerns of women in family enterprises, and have,
therefore, alienated many women.

Why do farm women appear willing to accept the restrictions
placed on them by their family consciousness? To understand the
position of farm women, it is necessary for us to examine more
closely the work on the public and private spheres, and to look at
the power relations in each of these spheres.

POWER: PUBLIC AND PRIVATE

One of the most illuminating arguments developed by feminists has been the work on the public–private split in society. As
capitalism developed, the modern urban nuclear family lost much
of its precapitalist productive role. Urban production now takes
place almost solely in the marketplace. Consequently, women's
domestic work has come to be devalued because it is unpaid and
because it is not geared directly to the marketplace. This association of women with the private sphere has also acted to devalue
women in themselves. Whereas some feminists see the association
of women with the private sphere as a changing historical development,[44] others see it as overriding and universal.[45] Whatever the
case, the biological, reproductive function of women has led to
their restriction and association with the private sphere, while
men, who are not privately constrained in this way, are ideologically viewed as being of the public sphere. Public power, then, is

almost exclusively male.

It is evident that the public face of agriculture is male, and that farming is seen as a male occupation, while farm women are viewed as farmer's wives or daughters. There are few women on agricultural decision-making bodies and few are employed in agricultural extension or advisory positions, although this is gradually changing. Like many women, farm women are constrained by their biological, reproductive function, and are ideologically consigned to the private sphere, despite the reality of what they do.

Radical feminists believe that women unconsciously collude in the acceptance of their subordination and oppression;[46] so, too, do the socialist feminists, who see it in Marxist terms as false consciousness. Poiner argues that women assent to their social inferiority because it accords them material advantage.[47] Women's collusion is generally explained by the socialisation of women, who have been taught from early childhood to accept their secondary status. They learn to accept that society is divided into public and private spheres, and that each has its appropriate gender role. Because public power is allocated exclusively to males, women experience gender as social inferiority.

A more important aspect of women's collusion and acceptance of their subordination is their private power in the domestic sphere. The private, informal power of women is a difficult concept for sociological analysis, because it is less visible than public power and has no relation to 'legitimate authority'.[48] However, within the private realm of the family, it is women's nurturing role which gives them influence. It is arguable that farm women could, potentially, hold more private power than urban women because of their integral role not only in the reproductive process but also in the productive process of their enterprise. The family agricultural enterprise depends on all household members for labour. In fact, the enterprise depends at all times on family formation and development for its survival. The farm woman, firmly entrenched in the productive sphere, in contrast to the urban housewife, holds enhanced private power because of her importance to the enterprise.

In noting that women are not considered as successors to the farm, Seena Kohl suggests that although one would expect this to lead to greater exploitation of women and lack of power and restriction of alternatives, in fact, it leads to farm women having wide alternatives and important power in the family enterprise because of the fusion of family and work.[49] This private power may explain the satisfaction most farm women express with their lot. They may, in fact, feel it is in their interests to support the ideology of male hegemony. As Janeway suggests '... When women cling to their traditional role, it is not primarily because they find masochistic pleasure in being dominated ... but because this role offers them power too: power in return for public submission ... Enough authority within their traditional place balances an external subordination that is not too wounding.'[50]

Farm women have a wide diversity of roles in their lives. As mentioned previously, a lot of what farm women do would be described as 'men's work' in an urban context, and so, farm women are not as ideologically constrained in their working lives as are many women. However, despite the fact that they are integrated into the productive side of the enterprise and hold enhanced private power, publicly farm women are unacknowledged. Males still control the resources and the public face of agriculture, and it is in men's interests for women to remain committed to 'feminine conservatism'.[51] Nevertheless, farm women report enormous satisfaction from the various activities they perform which have a productive focus, and while experiencing this satisfaction, they see little relevance for themselves in the widely publicised feminist call to abandon the family (or at least critically examine the restrictions it places on them) and to seek meaning through autonomy. In fact, feminism is seen as very threatening because it seeks to limit farm women's traditional sources of power and provides no obvious gains in exchange.

SUMMARY

T he marginalisation of women and their exclusion from Australia's history and culture has been aided by the androcentric nature of sociological theorising. The emergence of feminist theory in recent times has allowed the lives and work of women to be given significance. This woman-centred analysis has seen a focus on the areas of nurturing and intimacy, and a call to incorporate these virtues into public life. Far from repudiating early radical feminist theorising, there is a need to draw on the insights made by these early theorists in a renewed commitment to social change. Yet, feminist theorists have managed to alienate farm women, not least because of their selectively and widely reported comments concerning the role of the family. At the same time, farm women's unique circumstances have not been adequately treated by feminists. Primarily, feminists need to retreat from false universalism in order to incorporate the experiences of all women, including farm women.

Farm women continue to put the farm first and make considerable sacrifices to ensure the family farm survives, and, not unlike women of colour who give preference to race over gender, farm women tend to give priority to their farm family identity over gender. Farm women see the exploitation of the farm family unit by agribusiness and state policies in the marketplace, as well as the current disastrous returns, as a more immediate oppression and threat which overrides their own oppression as women.[52] This gender oppression is seen as less significant than the satisfaction gained from working together with family members, and so, the crucial nature of the current crisis in agriculture in forming solidarity amongst farm family members cannot be discounted. As well, women's labour is often rewarded by a strong sense of companionship with their spouse, which would be unusual in an urban setting, where work and home are separate spheres. It must also be realised that farm women have gained satisfaction from accumulating property to be passed on to the next generation. Feminism on the farm has, in fact, been described as being reflected by this sense of companionship and continuity of the family enterprise, ideas with which feminist theorists must come to grips.[53] 'For over one hundred years, [farm women] have demonstrated a form of feminism that reaches beyond any simple definition of autonomy or individualism — farming women have claimed the right to integrate work and family life with an enduring respect for the earth which is, after all, one sphere'.[54] Because of their socialisation, their lack of role models and their lack of interaction with other women, farm women see urban-based feminism as offering them little and, indeed, as threatening their unique position.

Not only has feminism alienated many farm women with its reported pronouncements, but the women's movement has had little impact in the bush because farm women have been very comfortable with the status quo. It appears that their subordinate public status has been offset by enhanced private power within their enterprise. However, as farm families are increasingly squeezed out of the marketplace, women (and men) may be becoming victims of exploitation as they attempt to juggle traditional expectations with increased workloads. Farm women may, in fact, increasingly become attuned to a feminist philosophy which understands where they are coming from and gives them direction to fight their exploitation. They may be becoming more aware of their exploitation, as well as their integral role in the economic survival of the family which does not tally with their subordinate public status. Farm women need to be made aware that their private power is not under threat from feminist theory, but that what needs to be challenged is their exclusion from the public sphere, their lack of control of resources and the lack of reward for their efforts.

We must not lose sight of the value of the work of feminist theorists in allowing a woman-centred focus to be adopted. Concepts such as patriarchy, ideology, gender and the sexual division of labour are useful in describing the constraints on women living in rural areas. With these ideas firmly in mind, I will now turn to an examination of the lives of farm women.

CHAPTER 3

THE CHANGING NATURE OF WOMEN'S WORK ON FARMS

I would have loved to have been a hairdresser or a florist ... I've missed out on that side of life.
67-year-old farm woman, southern New South Wales.

Increasing capitalisation of agriculture and technological advances have led to major shifts in the way the business of farming is conducted. While these changes have had an impact on all family members — with consequent shifts in the way labour is allocated — for women, they have meant extraordinary changes in the way they live their lives. To understand the impact on women and the changing nature of their work, we must examine the work of farm women earlier this century.

Studying women and their work from an historical perspective is not entirely simple: what is particularly irksome is the lack of recorded women's history. Much evidence about previous generations of women has been lost, and we are left to rely on anecdotal accounts. Studying women in agriculture is like looking into a black hole: accounts of women's involvement are very sketchy and, in fact, established agricultural histories provide little evidence of the significance of women's contributions. Official statistics are equally poor sources, because they have failed, and continue to fail, to accurately record the details of women's efforts. As a consequence, we must rely on sources, such as personal memories of older women, diaries, letters and newspaper accounts, and exhaustive academic studies for historical evidence of women's involvement in agriculture. Such sources have alerted us to the shape of the lives of the women of the squattocracy who were able to continue to aspire to an aristocratic way of life. However, for the majority of women engaged in farming, this is not an accurate picture. Academic studies which have given us a more detailed picture of the way of life for many women on farms include those of Marilyn Lake,[1] in an Australian context, and Deborah Fink, in a US context.[2]

Lake presents an historical account of soldier settlement in Victoria from 1915 to 1938. The exploitation of the soldier settlers and their wives is evident from Lake's work. She details the horrendously hard work in which women were engaged, which was supported by the rural press who exhorted women to be noble 'helpmates' to their husbands. However, contradictions in their situations were apparent, and it was difficult to be noble when feeling totally exhausted. During this period, the widespread development of the ideology of domesticity in Australia had resulted in middle-class women retreating to the home to provide the safe haven sought by idealistic politicians. Spurred on by the movement towards domesticity, farm wives, struggling with their double workload on the farm and at home, began to question the assumption that they should continue. Many suffered from a breakdown in their health or simply packed up and left. Lake cites the example of farmer Norris, who applied to the Soldier Settlers' Commission to sell his land, because 'the doctor had "ordered" him to keep his wife "away from the farm work"'.[3] Implicit in his plea was the fact that he could not manage without his wife's labour. The commensurate development of the notion of separate spheres and a domestic role for women, which was fostered by politicians and the media, and women's growing acceptance of a domestic role for themselves, must be seen against a background of back-breaking hard work for both rural and urban women. That women rushed to embrace the notion of their domestic place must be understood in the light of their need to escape the double load. That one result of their escape from this load was a rigid definition of a sexual division of labour seemed a small price to pay at the time.

There would appear to be a parallel situation occurring currently among farm women. Many farm women report feeling overworked, overtired and stressed. Jenny, a 38-year-old New South Wales farm woman with three young children, states: 'It's just becoming more and more demanding. Whereas he can't leave the farm and get a job elsewhere because someone has to run the farm, she can. So therefore it's just another thing that she has to do … It's just seems to be becoming insurmountable!' Modern farm women's work has again extended far beyond the household domestic sphere, as many work on and off the farm to acquire much needed income. However, women are no longer seeking a retreat to the domestic sphere, but argue for a more equitable sharing of responsibilities within it.

While there has been little attempt to reconstruct a history of farm women in Australia, it is possible to note from existing sources and from the accounts of older women the broader changes that have occurred for women. The telephone, better transport and electricity have profoundly affected the work of farm women within the lifetime of several of the women interviewed for this study. The effects of these developments should not be discounted, because they have acted to free women from many labour-intensive activities within the household, and have allowed them to be linked to the wider community with access to resources and services and, importantly, to off-farm employment.

Before electricity was introduced, farm women used such items as hand-operated cream separators and butter churns, wood cooking stoves, washboards and handwringers. Electricity enabled water to be pumped, homes to be heated other than by wood fires, refrigeration to be introduced, milk and cream to be separated other than by hand churning and produce to be frozen. It allowed the introduction of refrigerators, vacuum cleaners, electric stoves, washing machines, lights, clothes dryers, electric sewing machines, heaters and fans, toasters and kettles. The importance of this innovation in changing the labour of farm women cannot be underestimated.

The introduction of electricity is remembered with great awe by nine older women interviewed during the course of my research. Before this momentous event, the women remembered dealing with kerosene lights and kerosene refrigerators, wood stoves and coppers, wash tubs and drip safes, amongst other things. The women remember the hard, physical labour associated with these appliances — wood to be chopped, food to be preserved, clothes to be boiled, wrung, starched and blued, lamps to be filled and floors to be scrubbed (because carpets were impossible without a vacuum cleaner to clean them). These women remember the introduction of electricity as providing immediate relief. Joan reminisced about the impact of electricity on her workload. 'Less work, definitely less work … It was a relief to be able to just switch on the light rather than go and fill a lamp with kerosene and fiddle around with mantles … I definitely could relax more … it was a freer feeling all over.'

The changes to clothes washing brought about by having access to electric washing machines was the 'best thing' for some women, and certainly reduced their labour quite markedly. The freedom from household labour that electricity provided allowed women to escape the confines of the house, often to be drawn into on-farm and off-farm work.

Changes in transportation have also released women from confinement to the farm. Some women remember driving a horse and sulky to town. Cars have allowed women ready access to their towns for social activities and services. Access to supermarkets and department stores with cheap alternatives to subsistence products has freed women from many tasks associated with subsistence production.

Ready transport access has also put women in touch with off-farm employment. Yet, while improvements in transportation have been a bonus for farm women, it should be noted that 39 per cent of the women interviewed felt that the increasing cost of petrol was forcing them to reconsider and reduce the number of times they now left the farm.

Only a few women in the study were ever without the telephone, and its importance in linking women to their communities is vital. Its use as a social networking tool for women has been adequately documented by Ann Moylan in her Australian study.[4]

For farm women, being able to use the telephone broke down the barriers of their isolation and overcame the problems of distance.

PRODUCTION FOR CONSUMPTION AND SMALL-SCALE ENTERPRISES

A s a result of these technological developments, the work of farm women has dramatically altered. One of the most evident changes in their patterns of work has been the move away from subsistence production and the production of goods for consumption to a move off the farm to work for income to buy such items. My own research supports the findings of Fink about the nature of women's work on farms earlier this century.[5] Both studies demonstrate that older women produced much of their family's food and made most of the family's clothes. Women report having large vegetable gardens and orchards, butchering their own meat, milking cows, making butter, keeping poultry and making soap and other consumable products. Moyra, a 65-year-old New South Wales farm woman, who left school in her early teens when her mother died, reported:

> When I left school [in the late 1930s] I came home and I milked four cows and I used to get the milk up and I used to separate the milk and we made the butter. And that is why I think today is different … You kept a house on nearly nothing because you had your own chooks … your own milk and you would have your own butter and you would have your own cream and you would have your own eggs and you would have your own meat. And basically … it was basic food like meat, potatoes and pumpkin and something and custard.

As a result of women's subsistence production, the farm was freed from the obligation of buying such goods, and money saved could be reinvested in the farm and plant. As an indirect result of women's work, the farm thrived.

As well as their work in subsistence production, many farm women kept their own small-scale enterprises, which allowed them to generate independent income. Most commonly, these enterprises included egg production, butter and cream production, rearing poultry and other young animals such as lambs and calves. Many older farm women I spoke with reported the benefits of such enterprises for their families. Rosie, a 60-year-old retired farm woman, reported:

> I did have chooks, yes, when we were first married I had a hundred pullets, and we used to live off those pullets … We would pack say 15 dozen or 30 dozen eggs and I would take them to the Egg Board. I probably got about 12 pounds, and we really lived off that 12 pounds. … So that would have gone on for ten odd years … and it really was great, because it was one way that a woman always had a bit of cash in her hand…

Mary, a 73-year-old retired farm woman, was another who remembered the benefits of her own small enterprise.

> I started off my life on the farm with 20 chooks and that 20 chooks grew to a thousand … I looked after all those chooks … Oh it would be more, probably more than ten years, I really did … I used to sell the eggs to the Egg Marketing Board … and I used to sell the butter to the hotels in X… Well, it was very good. I furnished eventually all our home. All this furniture you see here, that's from my eggs.

Many older farm women tell similar stories. In fact, a recurring theme in their reminiscences is the sense of independence, pride and accomplishment and an enhanced sense of self-worth gained as a result of having run their own industries. Fink's report of US farm women engaging in similar small-scale production on their own behalf suggests this was a general trend among farm women earlier this century.[6] Yet, there appears to be no official record of their industries, and the resulting economic contribution they made to their enterprises, in the established agricultural literature.

The lives of older farm women were characterised by an acceptance of the notion of separate spheres and a sense of mutual respect between spouses, whose interdependent efforts ensured the family survived and thrived on the land. Gender-specific distinctions ensured that men were largely responsible for the work in the paddocks and that women took care of the home-based tasks. Each tended to accept their role according to the accepted prescriptions of the time, and that acceptance gave each a sense of surety. Yet, Fink notes that there was little real differentiation between the family tasks and enterprise tasks of women.[7] In fact, she suggests that a curious process of gender differentiation ensured that when women took responsibility for a particular enterprise, that enterprise was redefined from farmwork to household work. So, enterprises such as poultry and egg production were seen as household work rather than farmwork while ever women looked after them. While each respected and appreciated the work of the other, the integral nature of women's role was not appreciated outside the private realm of the family. The spheres were viewed as separate but not equal — women continued to be seen as subordinate and their work remained undervalued by the wider community.

Changes in the nature of farm women's efforts were brought about partly by the imposition of government regulations, which were introduced to monitor the production of eggs and dairy products on farms. Insensitive to the value of these industries for women, government departments adopted heavy-handed tactics which inevitably resulted in the closure of these industries. Rosie reports how this happened for her:

> When it finished was when they brought in that you had to register your chooks and they were five pence ... that came in the sixties ... Oh yes I was angry! The fellow came onto the place and asked me how many chooks did I have, and at that particular time I had about 55 and you were allowed, I think it was 25... before you had to register them. So he went down and counted them! And I said "Don't worry about counting them because I won't register them and that's it!" And that was it — I sold them.

The reasons for the regulation of small production units are vague. The subsequent development of large-scale production of these commodities suggests the state was working against small commodity-production units in favour of capitalist forces. Nevertheless, what these women's stories demonstrate are the unforeseen effects on women of the commercialisation of their products. It also challenges the notion that large-scale production is somehow better for the community. For example, because of research on vitamin D attributes, it has become possible to raise hens indoors by feeding them vitamin supplements, and as a consequence, large-scale, indoor battery-hen operations have developed where hens live their lives in small cages and never see daylight. These hens are also given large doses of antibiotics to ward off disease. While commercialisation of production and the development of capitalist units are seen as examples of progress, sometimes that progress can be questionable.

Nevertheless, the taking over and regulation of women's farm industries resulted in the loss of independent income for many. Sarah Whatmore's British study demonstrates that British women are still engaged in their own enterprises on farms.[8] She cites examples of women running bed and breakfast establishments on their farms, others who sell produce at roadside stalls and one who runs a butcher shop from the farm. The problems of distance make such ventures unviable in the Australian context and, in fact, women have moved away from subsistence production and cottage industries.

At the same time as this change was occurring, the development of cheap, factory-produced goods meant that clothes and goods previously produced on the farm could be bought at supermarkets and department stores. Better roads and faster transport made access to these goods easier for farm women. What many women now needed was a ready source of cash income to purchase the goods they had previously produced themselves. The farmhouse was changing from a site of production to a site of consumption. As a result, there was an escalating trend towards women moving off the farm to work.

THE DEVELOPMENT OF
CAPITALIST AGRICULTURE

R unning parallel with this redefinition of women's work on farms was the change taking place in large-scale agricultural production. Previously, production had been labour-intensive, with farms employing hired labour to help with the farmwork in cases where there was not enough family labour. A change towards capital-intensive agriculture has escalated over the last 25 years. Julian Cribb reports that 45,000 farm labourers left the industry in the 1970s.[9] This trend has continued and accelerated, with the result that rural towns based on agriculture are being depopulated. An indication of the effects of these changes is the number of banks and post offices being closed down in small rural towns at the present time.

Technological advances have led to increasing control over product inputs by agribusinesses and to what has been referred to as the 'technological imperative', or the need to continually pursue the latest innovations in order to maintain profits.[10] Geoffrey Lawrence states that 'this technological imperative means that the farmer has climbed aboard the agribusiness treadmill becoming in the process a sort of rural "junkie" hooked on agricultural chemicals'.[11] It appears that the 'technological imperative' and the development of capitalist agriculture have had, and will have, devastating effects on family farming and on the social relations of production. The immediate imperative for families is to increase the size of their holdings and/or to increase their production to cover costs, and in order to do this, they must acquire bigger machinery and make greater use of chemicals in cropping and animal husbandry. All these adaptations tend to be capital-intensive and replace previously labour-intensive practices, causing enormous structural changes in rural communities. The rationale behind the imperative is the need to increase production levels and to reduce the time taken to produce a product. However, the introduction of expensive inputs increases the cost–price squeeze on family farms, increases oversupply of products and necessitates a greater cash flow. The new technologies and practices have entered both crop and livestock industries, and include chemical control of weeds and pests; larger and more sophisticated machinery; and livestock technologies such as embryo transplants, artificial insemination and hormone implants. Farming families are finding the technological imperative in agriculture is a treadmill from which they cannot escape if they are to remain viable, and yet, the effects of this imperative on human health and the environment are questionable.

It must be conceded, however, that many of the new technologies have made life easier for farm families. Nonetheless, women express concerns about some farm practices, particularly the increasing use of chemicals in agriculture, and express the view that their production unit is powerless to arrest the process.

THE EFFECTS OF TECHNOLOGICAL CHANGE ON FARM FAMILIES

The introduction of technological advances in agriculture has had dramatic effects on the farming families investigated and farming families in general. As we have seen, these effects include the adoption of capital-intensive practices to replace labour-intensive strategies; the purchase of bigger machinery and more land; changes in cropping practices; a greater reliance on chemicals; changes in livestock-management practices; a need for a greater cash flow, which often necessitates working off the farm and/or borrowing money from banks; the need to work harder, longer and smarter; the need for ready access to technical information about farming; and the need for improved and more sophisticated bookkeeping. These points will be discussed separately.

The trend to larger, less labour-intensive farms has accelerated over the last 20 years. One result of this development has been the creation of a new 'rural underclass' of unemployed farmers and farmworkers needing state support.[12] In the cropping areas, for example, the increasing use of chemicals which allow direct drilling of seed, coupled with bigger machinery, has replaced the use of labour to work up land. Similarly, dramatic changes have occurred in livestock practices with, for example, the new chemical lice-control spray having replaced the labour-intensive plunge dips of yesteryear. The adoption of these new technologies by farming families has had a profound effect on their labour requirements and has led to the dramatic decline in farm labourer numbers. Many women are able to give examples of this process in action on their farms. Kristen reported an experience on her family's farm.

We had two tractors, which meant that we needed an extra man at sowing time, whatever. So we costed it all out and sold the two tractors privately, reduced the staff by one on a casual basis and bought a brand new [bigger] John Deere tractor, which might put us a little further into debt, but overall was a good business decision ...

Marie, an older farm woman, told a similar story. 'As we scaled down with staff, we gradually went into bigger and wider machinery, and that enabled us to do the same amount of cropping with less men.' One of the most obvious effects of capitalisation and the 'technological imperative' is the challenge to acquire new and improved machinery able to do more work at a faster rate. In fact, in the cropping areas, 81 per cent of women questioned stated they had upgraded and improved their farm machinery in the previous few years. Those who had not felt they could not afford to do so. In the mixed farming areas, 53 per cent of women reported a similar process of upgrading machinery. Susan, a farm woman living on a cropping farm, reported: 'Well, they've got a bigger header, and now we sow with an air seeder and that has depth-control monitors. And they spray with monitors — there's definitely a lot of advances in that way.'

The need to keep up with these advances does place families on a technological treadmill which is difficult to maintain but almost impossible to escape. As Barbara explained:

> Well, you really have to do that to ... to keep ahead. Well, not ahead but you have to keep abreast of things, because if you stick with the same tractor, in ten years' time, it is had it ... you're not going to get anything for your old tractor. You've really got to keep up ... because the cost of machinery is astronomical.

Julie corroborated this view: 'To keep your farm going and to keep ahead with things, you have got to keep updating the machinery and that is a lot of outlay.' The rationale behind this constant pressure to keep abreast of changes is the need to maintain and, indeed, increase productivity in order to remain viable. As Helen succinctly put it: 'You've got to get bigger and get over the ground quicker.'

The change in pace to the almost-manic dimensions of present-day farming was highlighted in my research by the accounts of older women with long memories of the pace of farming 40 to 50 years ago. Several, like Catherine, recalled the draughthorse days: 'Yes, because we weren't far from draughthorses when we started ... Before the war, there had been horses. There were still horses around and old tractors and machines. The type of tractors that we used were quite primitive by today's standards.' The changes within the lifetime of some women interviewed have been dramatic, and have seen farms metamorphose into technological business ventures linked to a world market.

The drive to maintain and upgrade machinery and farming practices has impelled an expansion in holdings to increase production and, in a number of cases, maximise the use of the new machinery. This trend towards expansion is evident in my research, with 22 per cent of women reporting land expansion during their time on the farm. For instance, Sonya, married 25 years, reported: 'I guess it was 2000 acres [800 hectares] when we were first married ... and now we have just over 5000 acres [2000 hectares].' Similarly, Janet, married 20 years, stated: '[My husband] and I personally have [expanded our land] twice since we have been married and we are leasing extra land at the moment, too.'

In order to maximise the use of new machinery, several women report husbands and sons taking on contract work. For instance, Helen echoed the words of many women when she reported: 'It had a big effect on us this year because we bought a big baler and [my husband] did a lot of contract work, which meant that he was away from the farm quite a lot — for probably a couple of months.' Women reported their husbands using their machinery to do contract stripping, baling, spraying or windrowing. This contract work accounts for the majority of the off-farm work attributed to the husbands of the women in this study, and is another aspect of the 'technological imperative' which impacts on the social relations of production on family farms.

While upgrading of machinery was widely reported, this process has been arrested during the rural commodity downturn and capital stocks are being run down. That this is a general trend is supported by the 1992 Australian Bureau of Agricultural and Resource Economics (ABARE) *Farm Surveys Report,* which states that the real stock of plant and machinery has steadily run down since 1983/4. Families across Australia are obviously struggling in their attempts to remain abreast of developments.

As well as expanding their land and holdings, families are changing their methods of farming. All the farm women questioned were asked about the reliance on chemicals in agriculture, and all reported that chemical intrusion into agriculture is a blanket development. All the women on cropping farms believe that their farms now rely on chemicals to maintain and increase production, while those on mixed farms note that the reliance on chemicals is, again, widespread. All noted some level of use, although six women reported (often unsuccessful) attempts to reduce or phase out chemicals. This encroachment of chemical control of weeds and insects into agriculture is, again, something which has occurred within the lifetimes of the older women interviewed, and represents the increasing control of agricultural inputs by agribusinesses. The introduction of such methods has occurred with little opposition as farming families strive to stay ahead of their creditors. Despite the views expressed by the women concerning the necessity of chemicals, very few felt comfortable with their use. Most felt the same way as Jean: 'I don't like chemicals. But in today's farming, they are a necessity — they absolutely are. But you know I don't like them. I don't think a lot of people do like them but they are just one of those things you have to use.'

The development of chemically based farming is one strategy that has developed to reduce land degradation, by replacing the overworking of land, and the time that land is taken out of production during a fallow period. Fiona remembered a different time on the land. 'Well, one time years ago you always fallowed your paddocks. You didn't put as much crop in. You fallowed your paddocks and then worked them ... but now they are more inclined to get it in with less working.' This was corroborated by all the older women. Rosie summarised the thoughts of many. 'I suppose it was because they used to fallow ground in October, November and leave it, you see. Whereas they got that way they couldn't leave that ground ...' Very few farms can now afford to leave land idle by fallowing.

Another reported reason for chemical means of production is the reduction in the amount of fuel needed to produce a crop. Miriam stated the economic rationale behind the move into chemically based agriculture. 'We usen't to use any chemicals at all, but now they don't use half the amount of fuel that they used to use. It is mainly chemicals.'

Women raised their concerns about chemical use in agriculture, including the unknown effects on the health of their male family members and fears for their own health, particularly when they were pregnant. Meg voiced the fears of many women about their concerns for their men. 'When you have a son who sprays on Saturday and walks in on Sunday and says, I don't feel well. Yes, I am very uncomfortable.' Carrie was another who expressed deep discomfort with the effects of chemicals on her sons. 'Oh, it worries me a great deal, particularly as the boys won't take precautions very greatly. I go to all those meetings and come home with all this information and tell them all about it and try and get them to take notice but they won't … They are very careless and this does worry me a lot.' Jenny was more in tune with the thoughts of the younger women, who worried about the effects on their unborn children.

> Well, it has its pluses and minuses. As far as land degradation goes, it is good because you are not overcultivating the land. But then I think everyone worries about the pesticides and herbicides you are absorbing. Obviously, we absorb a lot more than people in the cities do … I was really worried when I was pregnant.

This concentration on chemically based agricultural production has occurred despite the private fears and concerns of most farm women and many of their husbands. It demonstrates the degree of control over agricultural production by agribusinesses and the powerlessness of farm families to escape the 'technological imperative', despite concerns for their own health.

The changes that have occurred in livestock practices are less widespread and cause far less concern to the families involved. Changing practices include the intensive farming of pigs and other livestock; the development of feedlotting of animals; the use of embryo transplants; artificial insemination to manipulate livestock breeding; and the use of hormone implants to accelerate growth of animals. Again, these strategies are designed to accelerate and increase production, and to cut down on the 'socially necessary' production time supposedly fixed by nature.[13] Seventeen per cent of women reported that rather than expand their holding, they had intensified their livestock practices. The strategies adopted included the setting up of pig sheds, the introduction of cattle feedlotting and the development of sheep or cattle studs. As well, 19 per cent of women reported that embryo transplants, artificial insemination and/or hormone implants were practices adopted by their enterprise. These practices, and the development of chemical controls, are examples of 'appropriationism', or the attempt to subvert the importance of natural cycles to allow increased social manipulation of agricultural products.[14]

To maintain levels of technological innovation, farming families need access to a steady cash flow. This can be obtained by securing off-farm income or by taking contract work to maximise the use of machinery and attempt to cover its cost. The need for an increased cash flow may also lead families to increase production by sowing more crop, increasing livestock numbers, intensifying farming practices or expanding holdings. Increasing production, however, leads to increased costs and can also lead to oversupply, which results in reduced prices. Elizabeth noted: 'The pressure is on every dollar you spend. [It] has got to produce and you just can't waste a dollar on farm on just anything.' Chris was another who noted the pressure placed on her family to increase their cash flow. 'Well, at the moment we are putting in more crop to try and get as much money as what we were two or three years ago. We are not even getting as much money.' Sharon put it neatly: 'You have got to produce more to get less to keep going.' Often, then, the effects of a need for a greater cash flow leads families into debt and ties them into a situation where their production unit is controlled by the credit agency. Many women interviewed, particularly in the cropping areas, report that their enterprise is in a precarious financial position and that bank managers are in control of their farming program.

Farming families are, for the most part, working harder and longer for less return. As well, they are also needing to work 'smarter'. The need to adopt the correct strategy, to borrow at the right interest rate, to purchase the right machinery, to grow the right crops and so on, are decisions that families feel they have to make correctly every time or be jettisoned off the treadmill. When competing in a world marketplace with a less than level playing field, the 'correct' decision is often beyond the control of the individual farm families. A sense of powerlessness in the face of external realities often pervades the feelings of the women interviewed, and is evidence of the difficulties faced by farm families struggling to remain viable.

Farming families can no longer afford to isolate themselves from information about new technologies, markets, weather predictions or changing practices. This information is sought from several sources, including the *Land* newspaper and other rural newspapers, radio broadcasts, field days and demonstrations and the Department of Agriculture extension services. Women report that seeking information is a predominantly male task. However, 37.5 per cent of the women interviewed involve themselves in this task at some level by listening to the radio, reading newspapers and other publications and going to field days. In very few cases, women attend field days on farming practices by themselves.

The changes and developments in agriculture have also necessitated improved bookkeeping. It is no longer enough to work out figures 'on the back of an envelope' and take them along to the accountant. As Sue noted: 'I think people are more conscious of keeping good books ... than what they used to be. I think people like to see now on paper is this paying or isn't it paying. I think they are more conscious of that than what they used to be.'

The change towards acknowledging farming as a business venture which needs to be run along business lines was evident from the interviews conducted with farm women. It appears that farm women are integrally involved in ensuring that the farming industry develops a business focus.

THE EFFECTS OF TECHNOLOGICAL CHANGE ON FARM WOMEN

W hile all the points discussed above concern women as part of the enterprise unit, there are more personal and gender-oriented effects which impinge on women as a result of technological changes. One of the more obvious effects on women of the introduction of bigger machinery on farms is that it draws them into peripheral tasks associated with keeping the machinery going. These tasks include the 'go-fer' role, which involves providing a taxi service running to town for spare parts, transporting meals and helping shift machinery. Often, this continues when the men are doing contract work away from home. For example, Meg is employed full-time off the farm but still finds herself drawn into peripheral tasks associated with cropping and contracting.

We do some contract harvesting. Well, when this takes place, then I am involved because my car is a taxi. I am taking [my husband and son] to where they are working and getting calls on the two-way at 5.30. "You will have to stay there a while and pick us up at such and such a time", and I have to wait and pick them up from the silos — and I have to come in early in the morning. So inasmuch as our machinery is bigger, and it's enabling them to have some off-farm employment, I am more involved but not in their actual work.

As well as this peripheral involvement, women are left to see to the farm tasks when husbands are away contracting. Several women note that they are responsible for checking stock and coping with the day-to-day running of the farm while their husbands are away. Additionally, women are involved in keeping up to date with technological information and with maintaining and improving the bookkeeping practices of their expanding enterprises.

One dramatic effect of less labour-intensive agriculture on women is that they are no longer required to provide regular meals for hired workers. Another change which may be related to the retreat from labour-intensive farming is the reduction in the size of farm families. Farm families, like most Australian families, are much smaller than they were earlier in the century, and as a result, women are confined by childcare tasks for a much shorter period of time. There is a reduced period when they are unavailable for farmwork and they are freer to move off the farm to work. However, Rachel Rosenfeld notes the trend towards 'higher quality' children, which means that, while women have fewer children, they require a great deal more of women's time.[15] For farm women, this can mean driving long distances to sporting, music and school activities and taking part in other extracurricular events. Nevertheless, despite the need to undertake these tasks, women are much more able to move into the paid labour force.

CHANGING ROLES

W hile there have always been some women on large farms who are able to live a very comfortable life free from the demands of physical labour, the majority of women have always worked very hard on farms. Over the last 50 years, there have been great changes in the nature of the work women do on farms. The most significant change has been the move away from subsistence production, which resulted in women moving from their own independent but complementary sphere into the male sphere of agriculture and off the farm to take on paid work. The commercialisation of their products, the provision of cheap, accessible alternatives to their subsistence products, the development of capital-intensive agriculture and the reduction in the size of farm families have all aided this transformation.

Older women report feeling a great deal of satisfaction as a result of having had a productive role on the farm. Their efforts in producing subsistence goods and running their own small enterprises enabled them to provide most of the household's consumption needs. Younger women, whose work takes them into many areas both on the farm and off, do not always report the same degree of satisfaction. Yet, many are still working to cover the family's consumption costs by taking off-farm work. Despite the major changes in the type of work that farm women do, what has not changed for them is the hierarchical gender relationships which structure their lives. These will be examined in more detail in Chapter 4.

The following stories illustrate the different shape of the lives of farm women over the last 40 years. Mary's story demonstrates the enormous contribution of older farm women in the areas of home-based consumption tasks. In contrast, Ruth's story points to the disparate tasks younger women are performing and the difficulty they have in reconciling these tasks.

Mary's Story

Mary and her husband moved to their soldier settler block in 1947. For the first four years, while they established their block, they lived in a tin shed with a dirt floor and no electricity. Mary recalls washing in the open with a scrubbing board, cooking over an open fire and driving to town in an old army truck, their only means of transport. They moved into their house in 1951, and electricity was connected a couple of years later. In the meantime, they made do with a kerosene refrigerator and lamps and a wood stove. They lived without the telephone for 'many years'. Mary vividly remembers her early years on the farm. She did all the household and childcare work, she kept a big vegetable garden and grew an orchard, and she provided meals for workers for 35 years. She made jams and preserves, milked a cow, made butter and cheese, and made her own bread for a while. Mary even made many of her children's clothes. 'We had our own meat, milk, cheese, eggs, butter — everything that ... you needed, really. I made my own bread at one stage ... and I preserved all the while, we always had stacks of fruit ... then we used to make our own sausages ...'

Mary also had her own enterprises. She kept 1000 hens for more than ten years and sold eggs and butter in the local town. Her efforts enabled her to provide most of the goods needed by the family.

On the farm, Mary helped with all the sheep work and, in the early years, drove a horse and cart to pick up hay bales. However, with the arrival of tractors and machinery, she moved away from the cropping work. 'I didn't think it was my place to drive them.' Her husband employed hired labour to help on the farm, and this enabled her to concentrate on her home-based tasks. Over the years, Mary performed a great deal of voluntary work in her community at the school, the hospital and in the Country Women's Association (CWA) and church-based organisations.

Mary is now retired and living in the local town. She admits that she hates living in the town because she has nothing much to do. Leaving the farm was very traumatic, and she began to cry when remembering her work on the farm. 'I loved my 40 years on that farm more than anything in the world.' Nevertheless, Mary didn't ever describe herself as a 'farmer'. She was 'just a hard-working person'. It was obvious that Mary had gained a great deal of satisfaction from her work and that she felt she had made a very valuable contribution to her partnership and her farm. 'You just feel that you are doing a very good job — you just feel it!'

Ruth's Story

Ruth moved on to her husband's farm in the late seventies and has been farming for 15 years. She found it difficult to accurately describe what it is she does on the farm. This was because her work takes her into many different areas. She is totally responsible for household work and childcare, she works on the farm an average of about two days each week and she has a job in town for two days each week. Her income is used to buy the children's clothes and other household items. Ruth is very involved in community work, spending a few hours each week at the local school. She keeps a vegetable garden and an orchard, makes jams, keeps hens and sells a few eggs occasionally. She loudly disputes the idea that there are separate spheres, and asserts that the only reason women do the household work is because '... they apply themselves to the task more readily. I mean, they can't say they can't do it or they don't know how, they have to!'

Ruth's work on the farm varies with the seasons. She helps her husband with stockwork and will do some machinery tasks, although she keeps away from the bigger machines. During the sowing and harvest times, she is particularly busy with peripheral tasks. 'I can write whole days off ... in busy times. I can be anything from go to [a town 200 kilometres away] to get a part or go to [the local town] twice or feed five people or bed two extras down ... it varies a lot, but with the seasons, like a lot of things in farming.'

Ruth's husband does a lot of contract work with their machinery, and this can take him away from their farm for up to two months a year. During this time, Ruth sees to the day-to-day running of the farm. She feels competent at most tasks except the 'sheer gut-busting sorts of jobs I refuse to even attempt to do as just a self-preservation thing'. She is currently facing a dilemma about the direction of her own work. Her youngest child has gone to school and she is contemplating increasing her off-farm work hours. However, if she does this, the farm will have to employ someone to replace her and it really cannot afford to do this. This is a situation facing many farm women with the reduction in the numbers of farms able to afford hired labour. Women have become indispensable workers on many farms.

While she sees her husband as having the ultimate responsibility for decision-making, she feels her role as a sounding board is vitally important to competent management. As well as purchasing improved and larger machinery, she and her husband have expanded their holding and they 'work all the time to increase our productivity'. They use chemical control of pests and weeds, and have introduced hormone implants to improve their stock. She feels that farmers now must 'change their commodities [to suit the markets] and ... change their general awareness of marketing and politics and economics'. Ruth is much more aware of the world marketplace than Mary ever had to be. One thing that particularly upsets her is the perception of some outsiders about her status on the farm. Many outsiders ring the farm and ask to speak to the 'boss'. It makes her very angry that people in the community do not appreciate the depth of her understanding and knowledge of the farm.

Ruth feels that women's place in agriculture could be very great if '... men let it be. We need to educate them to an understanding that we actually have brains and could be their biggest asset.' While she is very committed to the farm, Ruth admits she will be not hurrying to encourage her sons to take over, because she feels the future for farming is very insecure. She enjoys her life on the farm, but lacks the same sense of certitude about her role that Mary expressed.

CHAPTER 4

HOW FAMILY SHAPES WOMEN'S LIVES

> I don't believe there are women's jobs and men's jobs. I think who-
> ever sort of fits to do it — or whatever is suitable for a particular family.
> I think that men and women are capable of doing either jobs.
> *30-year-old New South Wales farm woman.*

F arming families are different from the majority of urban
nuclear families. For farming families are not only a kinship
grouping, they are also an economic unit whose members work
together to produce their goods for the marketplace. Related by
birth or marriage, farm families are business partners, live together, work with each other, and have to cooperate closely for the
farm to remain efficient and viable. It is this 'interpenetration of
kin and capital'[1] or the 'integration of the farm system and the
family system within the larger world of market relationships'
which makes farming families unique.[2] The intersection of these
two worlds structures the relations between family members and
social relations of production, and shapes the way the partici-
ve and work. For farm women, the nature of the farm fam-
ment of which they are a part dictates the very texture

ilies are not undifferentiated sites where all mem-
they are structured around gender relations

which allow men to be dominant both within the family and within the production process. Because of the practice of farms being passed from fathers to sons (patrilineal inheritance), it is predominantly men who own the resources of agriculture and who control the way farms are managed. For women, this results in a narrow definition of their legitimate activities. The resulting sexual division of labour sees women taking responsibility for domestic labour and men controlling farm labour. This is seen as the 'natural' order, and the separate roles are reinforced in rural communities by rural media. Further, this gender division of tasks devalues women's work both within the family and the community, while men's work is accorded greater prestige and value.

FAMILY LABOUR

Yet, farm family arrangements have persisted over time because they are flexible and have advantages over other types of systems. For instance, farm families provide a ready source of available labour that can be drawn upon in busy times; women and children are often called upon to work more intensely in times of busy seasonal activity. This sometimes dubious advantage gives farm families an edge over corporate concerns based on waged labour. Yet, this edge has resulted in a level of exploitation of all family members. It is not unusual for men and women to work very long hours with rarely a break away from the farm. It is a level of exploitation which workers in other industries, protected by unions and award conditions, would find difficult to accept. It is, nonetheless, this ability of farming families to exploit themselves which has enabled their survival.

Another distinguishing feature of farming families is their ability to drastically reduce their standard of living in order to survive for relatively long periods with little or no profit. The fact that average broadacre farms have had negative incomes for eight of the last 16 years is an indication not only of their straitened circumstances but also of the tenacity of many farm families.[3] That family farming continues to be the dominant form of agricultural production demonstrates the ability of families to adapt to changing circumstances. Their gendered structure has ensured that land remains within the family and that skills are preserved through generations.

Farm women have supported and facilitated farm family arrangements, and their role in transferring land from generation to generation of males is crucial. Family farming has provided rewards for women in the form of occupational identity and opportunity for personal fulfilment. Yet, their interdependency with farm men, essential to successful family farming, does not necessarily translate into equality.

FARM FAMILY ARRANGEMENTS

D espite the support of farm women for family farming, a brief look at farm family structures demonstrates the restrictions such arrangements place on the autonomy of farm women. Women's power, or lack of it, often depends on the family or kinship arrangements around which the farm is organised. The farm family is often part of an extended family arrangement involved in a financial partnership. Some families are involved in brothers' partnerships, others are in extended family partnerships with two or more generations, all of which can impose an intolerable strain on the women involved because their labour contributions go unrecognised, their decision-making power is negligible and their financial security is marginal.

When the family farm has been inherited from the husband's family, which is most often the case, the wife can be made to feel marginal during business negotiations. This is an often-repeated complaint voiced by farm women who may be dependent on their fathers-in-law. It is not unusual for a male farmer to retain ownership and control of the business until well into old age. As a result, sons working on the farm may have little autonomy until they reach their forties or fifties. Often, these sons are not paid a wage but are expected to keep working with the expectation that they will eventually inherit. As a result of the father's control, there may be two or three generations of family living and working on a farm. Such situations can be very difficult for all concerned: sons lack independence, income security and autonomy; for daughter(s)-in-law, it can also mean being accountable to their father-in-law for their spending or the way they allocate their time. As Jenny, a 27-year-old farm woman, reported:

> If there was something to be done, you were expected to be home. But they never let you know when you were supposed to be there to help. So you always got into trouble because you were either picking up a kid at pre-school or doing something and you always got into trouble … My father-in-law, see, he's a great one. You're supposed to read his mind!

Middle-generation women who have no legal stake in their home and farm, such as Jenny, face difficulties, and although their husbands may have a legal partnership, they are equally powerless and dependent on the autocratic rule of their father.

INTERGENERATIONAL PARTNERSHIPS

Jenny's Story

Jenny is married with two boys aged six and four. She left school after year 10, as did her husband. She has been on the farm with her husband, father-in-law and mother-in-law for eight years. She and her husband and children live in a cottage near the house of her husband's parents, and the farm partnership includes her father-in-law, mother-in-law and her husband. The 930-hectare farm on which they live is owned by her father-in-law, and produces predominantly grain crops with some sheep and cattle. The farm has had a negative income for the past few years and their debt has escalated.

Jenny has recently started operating her own small business in the local town in partnership with another woman. She works six days a week in the town, and it is predominantly her income that supports her immediate family. Her husband takes some off-farm work, when he can get it, doing rouseabouting in shearing sheds, driving tractors and doing contract work. It is Jenny, however, who is responsible for most of the housework at her home, and she overcomes some of the problems by doing all the family's washing at work. Although her mother-in-law provides some of the family's meals and often looks after Jenny's children, Jenny does all the cleaning and other household tasks on her day off. She has had to curtail some of her voluntary work in the small community in which they live, but she is still president of the local public school Parents and Friends, secretary for the Football Ladies' Auxiliary, a member of a sporting club, a volunteer for Meals-on-Wheels and goes regularly to her son's school to help with reading. She is able to manage this by employing hired labour in her small business during the times she is doing community work, but she has cut back on her own leisure activities. She no longer plays sport, although she used to regularly play netball and indoor cricket, and she has very little time for visiting friends.

Jenny states that her main reason for working off the farm is to gain much-needed funds. However, she still claims that 'a close second [reason] is independence from a very close family'. Her off-farm work prevents her from getting very involved in farm tasks at present. However, she pointed out that farm tasks are sometimes saved for her day off in order to make use of her labour. On her last day off before the interview, she had spent the day lamb-marking. She is still heavily involved in peripheral tasks, such as collecting parts from the town, transporting men and machinery from job to job, and cooking meals for them at work and running them to where the men are working. She and her mother-in-law are responsible for the farm books, despite her own lack of any legal status in the farm. In fact, her father-in-law felt she had been responsible for a misunderstanding with the bank just before the interview. As a result, her father-in-law had:

> ... come in [to her shop] and yelled at me over something that the bank had done ... He yelled and carried on and I chucked a complete and total ... I mean in *here* in front of reps and things. I chucked a complete and total wobbly and rang up home ... He came back to town and apologised which was a total turnaround because it was so out of character ...

Before Jenny opened her small business, her husband received a minimal weekly wage from his father. Since Jenny has been working, this wage has stopped without any discussion with her husband and herself, although, as she says, 'the farm can't support any sort of income now'. Decisions on the farm are made almost solely by her father-in-law with some input from her husband. She has very little say about farm practices at all, and being from a nonfarm background, reports feeling disturbed by some practices. For example, 'When I was pregnant, especially with the spraying, it used to get to me, and there was one pregnancy where they had the aeroplane out — they couldn't get on the ground ... and [my husband's] the one who's sucking all those chemicals in and that gets to me a bit ... but there's nothing we can do about it.'

Jenny feels that their standard of living has declined considerably. They cannot afford a new car, a holiday or even a badly needed new heater for their house. She identifies herself as a small business manager, and has never called herself a farmer because she 'didn't ever really do all the things a farmer does'. Nevertheless, she sees women's place in agriculture as 'more important than ever'. Jenny foreshadows no future on the farm for her sons, although she would dearly love her eldest to take over one day. In the meantime, she will encourage them to remain at school at least until they finish high school.

The idea of feminism does not excite Jenny, although she admits to liking her independence. As she says, 'You can be your own woman and still be on a farm. It depends on which way you interpret yourself.' It appears that Jenny has dealt with her in ferior position on the farm by taking on a more visible role in her community. Her off-farm work and her high profile in community organisations have allowed her to achieve a measure of autonomy commensurate with her obvious interpersonal skills.

BROTHERS' PARTNERSHIPS

Sometimes, farm family arrangements include two or more sons. In such cases, there may be two or more families living on the farm and brothers working together in partnerships. Such situations are fraught with difficulty and rarely proceed amicably. Women in such arrangements may be answerable to or dependent on their brother(s)-in-law, and most report feeling frustrated and marginalised.

Robyn's Story

Robyn is 35 years old, married with a girl and two boys aged five, three and one. She comes from a farming background and had been on her farm with her husband for seven years at the time of the interview. The farm on which she lives is 730 hectares and is owned by her father-in-law. The operation of the farm is controlled by the partnership which includes her father-in-law, her husband and two of his brothers. The farm produces cereal grains and sheep. Robyn has a university degree and works part-time in the nearest large town, which is 50 kilometres away. Her husband did not complete high school. While Robyn works off the farm three days a week, a teenage girl from the neighbouring town comes in to mind the children.

Robyn is responsible for most of the housework, although since she has been working, she has had to give up her gardening and making clothes for her children. She counts as her leisure activities going off the farm to work and working the horses on the farm. Her voluntary work off the farm has recently increased since her daughter began school this year. She is involved in several organisations, including the local Show Society, the school, the preschool and the Agricultural Bureau. Robyn has worked off the farm almost constantly since she was married, except for short periods after the birth of each child. Her income goes to pay the babysitter and most household expenses. Nevertheless, she states very strongly that she is working for personal reasons, which enhance her self-esteem, and is looking to develop her career, despite the fact that she feels she is overqualified for her present position.

Robyn has little involvement in farm tasks other than some stockwork and peripheral tasks, such as transporting her husband and brothers-in-law around the farm and errand-running to town. This is a situation that frustrates and annoys her, particularly as she was used to working on her father's farm before her marriage. She described the partnership in the following way:

There are three brothers in the partnership, each brother, then, for tax purposes, is in partnership with his wife, but basically, the wives don't have any input into the business ... One of the reasons that led me to look for work was that when I first married and came here ... I wanted to help on the farm, but that really didn't work out. I definitely felt alienated then and looked for off-farm work so that I had something for myself ... The wage provided from the business is definitely not adequate to live on this year ... and I may even have to look at getting extra work later in the year.

Interestingly, the wage is decided at a family meeting to which the women are invited but where they don't feel they can speak up. Before this year's meeting, she urged her husband to say they needed some more money, but it didn't happen. The partnership is controlled tightly by her father-in-law. As Robyn notes: 'The boys [husband and his brothers] are at a stage of life, particularly the older ones, where they want independence and they would like to have spoken to their father about it, but he doesn't want to split the dynasty sort of thing. He actually still owns it, it's his and they rent the land.'

The father-in-law in consultation with Robyn's husband and brothers-in-law makes all decisions about the farm and none of the wives is involved in this process. Robyn does not feel that her input to the farm is important, and feels her husband does not see her as important outside the household. She also feels that others off the farm, such as the bank manager and the accountant, see her as irrelevant to its operation. This makes her feel very 'low' and 'irate'. Although Robyn doesn't identify herself as a farmer, she struggled to find an appropriate description before she came up with 'administrator'. Nevertheless, she feels that women have a huge input into farming, one that she described as 'unrecognised', and that they make 'better financial managers' than most farm men. Despite this, she does not closely identify with feminism, although, 'Years ago, before I was married I was probably a great supporter of feminism and equality for women.' She is discouraged by 'media portrayal of them as being over radical'. 'Anyway,' she concludes, 'if the men aren't prepared to change, it would be very hard for the women to achieve anything.'

WOMEN IN PARTNERSHIP
WITH HUSBANDS

Women who begin farming alone with their husbands, free from outside interference, report a great deal of satisfaction and personal autonomy as a result of their work on the farm. Without the constraints of extended family partnerships, women are able to involve themselves in the work of the farm and become attuned to the land and its potential. Rhonda's story is presented here to demonstrate the way women are able to commit to their farm and their industry when they feel they are in an equal partnership. Yet, despite her personal arrangements, Rhonda still feels responsible for household and family work and feels marginalised away from the farm.

Rhonda's Story

Rhonda is 31 years old, married with three children. She and her husband own their 605-hectare grazing farm, which they purchased eight years ago after working hard to save enough money for a deposit. They divide the farmwork so that Rhonda does all the cattle work and her husband does all the sheep work. They tend to share machinery driving tasks. Her husband does the maintenance tasks and she does the books, and both partners go to markets to buy and sell their stock. Because of their equal commitment and input to the farm, they also share the farm decision-making. Having young children, Rhonda has had to adjust her way of doing things on the farm. 'I have never been able to get out of anything because I was pregnant. You know, lugging the baby around on the back of a bike or a ute or whatever has just meant that you change your tactics at doing things.'

Despite her involvement on the farm, Rhonda reports she is 80 per cent responsible for the household and family tasks. She keeps an extensive vegetable garden, preserves fruit and vegetables and makes some of her children's clothes. As well, she is currently doing a university degree by distance education and hopes eventually to find some work off the farm. At the time of the interview, Rhonda was involved in a number of local community organisations, including the local school P and C, and had held a number of executive positions in these organisations. She is also a member of Landcare, a group which fosters care and concern for the sustainability of land.

Rhonda has an extensive knowledge of the farm and its workings. She notes that they have invested in a great deal of land improvement, including dams, fences, trees, erosion-control measures and pasture improvement, in their eight years on the farm. Yet, in spite of her extensive knowledge and joint ownership of the farm, Rhonda is 'pretty cross' that people who ring the farm usually ask to speak to her husband. As she notes:

We [women] tend not to be taken seriously. [As children] we are not taken out to the shed to see what a machine looks like pulled down, or we miss out on our apprenticeship fairly regularly, and I think there is a huge wall of sexism and chauvinism amongst businesses surrounding farming, so it is very hard to be taken seriously.

Despite not being taken seriously by some outsiders, Rhonda is ambitious about the extent of her future contribution to agriculture through agripolitics. Once she has attained her degree, she hopes to significantly increase her involvement in the public side of farming. Her enthusiasm is refreshing, and agriculture will gain much if she is allowed to contribute to agripolitics. Farming organisations can only benefit from young committed farmers such as Rhonda. Yet, the obstacles facing her will be enormous. She is aware that she has a battle on her hands. 'I don't think the industry realises the potential of involving the other half of the industry. They are missing out on all that brain power, all that thinking power, and people power.'

Rhonda feels that she is a feminist in her own way, although she finds it difficult to define feminism. 'If it is because we want to wear trousers the same as the men and take over the things that were traditionally theirs and become very aggressive about it, well, I am not happy about it. As far as seeking to be valued as an equal with other men [sic], I think that it is very important and it's a fight that I will be part of forever.'

Women such as Rhonda are the hope for the future of agriculture. Her self-esteem and commitment are a result of her sense of equality within her farm enterprise. It remains to be seen whether such women are allowed to achieve their ambitions of contributing their wisdom and experience to their industry bodies.

WOMEN WHO FARM ALONE

Only a small percentage of women are farmers in their own right, and this often only comes about through death of a spouse. Women who are farmers are most likely to be widowed, single or relieved of their housekeeping or childbearing responsibilities.[4] In fact, women are not often socialised to be farmers; rather, they are socialised to believe that their work in the home is their most important work.[5] Women's involvement in agriculture has been, and is, limited by the patriarchal nature of family farms such that when women live with men, the men usually control the enterprise. The most common way for women to inherit land is when they are widowed. Widowhood has been called the most powerful time in a farm woman's life, because it may be the only time she achieves autonomy in her productive life.[6] The husband's death transforms the woman from unpaid agricultural labourer or homemaker into a legitimate 'farmer', and her ability to make the transition successfully is evidence of the artificial nature of the patriarchal restrictions women face. Women who had previously had very traditional roles were able to take an active role in agripolitics when their status changed. By contrast, many widows who have experienced control of their farm and who are subsequently displaced by sons find the experience devastating. Kathleen's story is included to illustrate the way changing family circumstances impact not only on women's identity and their work role but also on the way a woman is perceived within the community.

Kathleen's Story

Kathleen is 63 years old. She has been widowed for 23 years, and has three grown children, the youngest of whom, a son, and the eldest, a daughter, work on the farm with her. She had three years of high school before leaving to work on the farm with her father. She has, in fact, never worked off the farm. Kathleen now owns the 2025-hectare farm, and has a partnership arrangement that includes all her children and herself. She produces grain crops and has some sheep and cattle, and she employs three workers to help the family run the farm.

When Kathleen married in the 1950s, her husband bought into the farm. He became the farmer and she retreated to the house to rear the children. She produced most of their food during their marriage, growing vegetables and fruit and milking a house cow, and she made most of the children's clothes. After 13 years of marriage, her husband died, leaving her with the three children under twelve. As she puts it, 'He was buried on a Monday and by Friday I was very, very involved in the farm.' She employed a live-in housekeeper to help with the children and they shared the household tasks. Kathleen took on the full-time running of the farm but still performed such domestic tasks as cooking for shearers. At the time of the interview, she shared domestic tasks with her eldest daughter.

Because of Kathleen's farmwork involvement, she has had little time for off-farm activities. She was not involved in voluntary organisations but did occasionally manage to play tennis and golf. She has always employed hired labour on the farm, so has never driven machinery, preferring to be involved in the stock side of the enterprise. Interestingly, Kathleen sees her youngest child, and only son, as the heir to the farm, despite the fact that her oldest daughter also works on the farm. She accepts that men are destined to be farmers and that her daughter will probably marry. Community censure may have aided this traditional view, although she herself has never experienced a problem. She did, however, remember the difficulties her son had when he returned to the farm. The perception of locals was that he should now be the farmer.

> When [my son] left school, people used to say "Who runs the place, you or your old woman?" And I used to get so wild ... I said, "When you stop going to the pub and hearing 30 other people and listen to me more, you'll get on better." So we had a period which was difficult ... because everybody seemed to want to tell him what to do and that didn't suit me ...

Kathleen sees her son as the farm production decision-maker now. She has, in fact, facilitated this shift. Earlier in her life, she saw decision-making pass from her father to her husband, then to herself. One of her concerns is that her son is now using chemical sprays where she would have used other methods.

When Kathleen was married, she identified herself as a housewife, despite being a legal owner of the land. After her husband died, she identified herself as a farmer and, as a consequence of this, she had no qualms about regularly attending the New South Wales farmers' meetings in the local town, even though she was the only woman there. She also went as a delegate to the conventions in Sydney on a number of occasions.

Since her son has virtually taken over control, he now attends. Despite her years on the farm, she does recall some men treating her as if she knew little about farming. 'This man came from the Department of Agriculture ... but he treated me as though I didn't know anything ...'

Kathleen has obviously had a rewarding life on the farm. Despite the tragedies that have beset her, she has succeeded in what she calls a 'man's world'. The way she has lived and worked has been shaped by her relationships with men. As a wife, she played a traditional role; as a widow she had legitimacy and public visibility as a farmer in her own right. She does, however, identify herself as conservative and tends to support the existing male-dominated nature of farming.

WOMEN WHO INHERIT FARMS

There are a very few women who inherit farms. Those who do are subject to intense scrutiny by the rest of the community. These women report that it is much more difficult for them to succeed because of the difficulties imposed from outside. For instance, lone farm women have greater difficulty borrowing money or they may be subjected to criticism from other women. Economic structures still militate against women's full participation, and, in fact, banks have acted in the past to restrict women's access to working capital. Financial assistance can be difficult to obtain for any beginning farmers, but if the new farmer is a woman, the banks can be very sceptical. Deborah, for example, a woman farming alone, described difficulties trying to access credit. 'There was one particular time when we [mother and Deborah] wanted to borrow money for sheep, and he [bank manager] said we would have to lie and say that we wanted machinery because they wouldn't lend me the money for stock ... Maybe they figured we weren't going to be good judges of stock or not going to make any money.' It is not only banks which may exhibit this prevailing view of male dominance but also machinery companies, stock and station agents and accountants — all of whom are essential to a successful farm enterprise.

SUMMARY

W omen's subordinate role in agriculture is maintained by the patriarchal social relations of family farming. Because farm families operate as an economic unit as well as a kinship grouping, they are different from the vast majority of nuclear families. Consequently, much of the sociological theorising about family is not relevant in the farm family situation. For women who usually marry into a farm family, their position is secondary and their place as wife is given strong ideological support in rural areas. As Sarah Whatmore notes, '... in a very material sense women's position on the farm and in "the family" is founded upon an acceptance of profoundly unequal gender identities and inequitable terms of entry into the labour process'.[7] Because women who threaten the gender order risk threatening their relationship, there are very good reasons for women to consent to their subordination. The structure of the farm family shapes the very nature of the farm woman's life. If the farm is owned by her father-in-law or in partnership with her husband's brothers, she will remain marginalised within the family and the business for much of her life. Women who begin farming with their husbands, free from outside interference, report far greater autonomy than women involved in extended family arrangements. Widowhood is often the time when farm women experience the most autonomy. It is evident that the type of family situation that a farm woman is involved in dictates the way she will interact within the family, on the farm and in the community where she lives.

CHAPTER 5

WHO'S GOT THE POWER?

... more women have to get into high places. I honestly believe that women have not done enough. Their potential hasn't been fully realised because men are blocking them.
35-year-old New South Wales farm woman.

T his chapter will examine the power differential between men and women within farm families, and within agriculture generally, to demonstrate the limits placed on women by the social relations in farming. We have seen how women in farm families are restricted and confined to a narrow definition of their role on the farm, a role very much structured by the nature of the family arrangement. Their secondary position as farm wife is reinforced by family members, the media and significant others off the farm. Women collude in their own subordination because such collusion affords them significant emotional and financial benefits. Should women fail to consent to their unequal gender identity, they risk losing the emotional support of their marriage and they may threaten the viability of their enterprise.

Their collusion is generally explained by their socialisation, because women have been taught from early childhood to accept their secondary status. They learn to accept that society is divided into public and private spheres and that each has an appropriate gender role. As a result, women continue, albeit grudgingly, to fulfil the expectations of other family and community members. Rumblings of discontent about the inequitable division of domestic labour are heard from farm women, yet they continue to perform the role expected of them. That men are aware of their power to enforce the established order is evident from the comments of farm women. One 24-year-old farm woman stated:

As [my husband] said when we first got married, he said, "You have the house, you can do whatever you want in the house … it doesn't bother me … that's your decision." You know if I wanted to make any major changes then that's fine with him. Because he said, "You're the one that's in it all the time and you've got to make it practical for you to work in", and he said, "I've got the farm". So I think he was trying to tell me, "Don't tell me what to do out there".

This man was clearly defining the limits as he saw them, limits which he expected his wife to maintain and which are enforced by rural ideology and community expectations. The threat of retribution or community disapproval is enough to ensure women continue to perform their subordinate role as the farm wife.

PRIVATE POWER

Yet, we have seen in Chapter 2 that women may collude in their own subordination because of their private power in the domestic sphere.[1] The farm woman, firmly entrenched in the productive sphere, holds enhanced power because of her importance to the economic viability of the business. Women are aware of their enhanced status within the enterprise; most see this resulting from their incorporation into legal arrangements involving the farm (should this be the case), changing expectations for women, changing male attitudes, their involvement in farmwork, their off-farm work and independent income, and their control of bookkeeping within the enterprise. The following quotes from farm women interviewed during the course of my study illustrate the awareness women have of their own power.[2]

I think women today have got more power — if they choose to use it — within a relationship. I think that is more of a result of more legal power, I mean they just have more power. And I think any thinking woman uses it.

I think that was a big thing with women on the farm is that they were so powerless for the social reasons — that generation didn't get divorced ... But I think the fact that I have a choice of employment and income that is away from the farm, certainly this empowered me one hell of a lot that if I didn't choose to stay here or whatever, that I could go!

I think probably past generations took their role as a foregone conclusion that they would have masses of kids and did what they were told ... Oh, I think I have a stronger role!

I think it's just the attitude of the males. Now they accept women for what they are.

These positive assertions of their own power were echoed by many women and demonstrate an awareness of their own improved circumstances as well as changing societal attitudes.

DECISION-MAKING

H owever, these changes in private relations of power within the relationships between husbands and wives have not resulted in increased involvement for women in decision-making on farms. Farm families must, of necessity, make decisions concerning their productive enterprise, which focus on the need to generate economic resources to support the family. They may rely on off-farm income, but, they also generate income from their interdependent efforts as a productive unit. They must make decisions about the way economic resources are divided between household and enterprise and about the day-to-day running of the farm. In my own study of farm women in New South Wales, women reported that they have little say in farm production decisions regardless of their legal status, farm background, educational level or any other variable. In fact, only 13.6 per cent of women felt they had a joint role in farm decisions. The married women variously described their input as 'a backstop', 'a sounding board', 'a devil's advocate', 'a support' or 'non-existent', 'minimal', 'limited', 'nothing' and 'no input'. Women whose husbands were involved in partnerships were particularly isolated from decision-making. Many described planning sessions from which they were excluded which might occur 'around the table at morning teatime' at their mother and father-in-law's home. Most of the women saw their involvement as being available to help their husband sort out his ideas. As one farm woman stated: '... he will sometimes talk to me about them. It is not always necessary for me to make intelligent comments back. It is just so that he gets a chance to air them and think about them.'

Responses of women to further questions about decisions within the household and family reveal a gradation of involvement in decision-making, from very little input into production decisions to shared involvement in major household purchases, and major decisions concerning children to nearly total responsibility for incidental decisions. Responses reveal that women have little power and control within the family production unit and share power within the family.

FARM ORGANISATIONS

A way from the farm, women are virtually absent from public arenas of power in agriculture. Their reluctance to be involved in the public sphere is usually explained by a lack of time and resources. While these are serious constraints, they have not prevented women from undertaking a great deal of voluntary work, which also takes time and resources. Their absence from the political arena has far more to do with the nature of the organisations themselves, their structures and the reluctance of such organisations to accept and acknowledge women. In my research, only 12.5 per cent of women reported being actively involved in agripolitics. Despite the fact that they are integrated into the productive side of the enterprise and have a sense of their enhanced private power, farm women are invisible publicly.

The lack of acknowledgment of women's concerns and interests by many farm organisations was made evident to me when I attended a series of meetings for farm women in Wagga Wagga, New South Wales, in October 1990, convened under the auspices of the powerful New South Wales Farmers' Association. It became apparent that the set agenda, which focused on commodity issues, was not addressing the more pressing issues for farm women. Little time was allotted at each meeting for women to voice their intense concerns about the withdrawal of their eligibility for the family allowance (a payment to women), and their problems of coping both with stress in their family relations and with no available money. The result of the avoidance, or neglect, of these issues was a stinging and prolonged outburst by many women at the final meeting. The New South Wales Farmers' Association was roundly criticised for daring to make a submission to the federal government concerning the family allowance without consulting the women themselves. The male organisers of the meetings found the criticism difficult to understand, demonstrating their lack of awareness of the difficulties women are experiencing in maintaining and supporting their families. This incident indicates both the developing consciousness of farm women and the failure of male-dominated agricultural organisations to come to terms with women's experiences.

Those women who have involved themselves in agripolitics are often the only women attending meetings, and they struggle against attitudes which exclude them. Significantly, women who are or had farmed alone for some period of time are more likely to be involved in agripolitics. Many women who had previously had very traditional roles before widowhood were able to take an active role in agripolitics when their status changed, and they were viewed, and viewed themselves, as the farmer.

However, most women report they are simply not interested in traditional farm organisations for various reasons. These reasons tend to vary with age: older women usually view these organisations as men's domain and related to his job. The lack of time because of family responsibilities and off-farm work is the reason given by most younger women for their lack of involvement. Others involved in partnership arrangements mention their feelings of alienation from agriculture which prevent them taking an interest in the political side of farming. This alienation brought about by marginalisation in family arrangements is a very important issue for farm women, and must be understood as a factor which prevents women putting themselves forward in agripolitics. Furthermore, the awareness of the continuing patriarchal structure of many such organisations prevents many women getting involved. In fact, many women note the need for a women's organisation that will allow them the freedom to pursue their political ambitions.

The barriers to women's involvement in traditional organisations and the current crisis in agriculture have, in some cases, led to the development of alternative female organisations. Organisations such as Women Involved in Farm Economics (WIFE) and American Agri-Women have developed in America, while groups such as the Women's Rural Action Committee in New South Wales, Women for Dairying in Victoria, the Sugar Wives' Action Group in Queensland, the Esperance Rural Survival Group in Western Australia and, of course, the Country Women's Association have mushroomed in Australia. Some are more enduring than others. More recently, the Farm Women's Network has developed in Victoria and New South Wales and promises a solid political base for farm women.

It is important to note that the consciousness of farm women has been shaped by their identification with the farm enterprise and the tasks they perform. In the past, they have overlooked their own oppression as women to focus on the problems associated with family farm survival. Their strong identification with the family-centred production unit causes them to react to domestic and foreign policies and economic conditions which threaten the survival of the family farm rather than to issues of gender inequality. 'In the nineteenth and again in the twentieth century, the themes of farm women, individually and as members of movements and organisations, have been family welfare and farm economics.'[3]

Farm women tend to support policies that will preserve the family farm, policies such as lower interest rates and price supports. As Gretchen Poiner suggests, '... they are satisfied by their efforts to return prestige to the whole family, but especially to men'.[4] Political action on their own behalf has been difficult, if not impossible, given the image of rural women within the male-dominated system of agriculture. However, there is evidence to suggest that this is changing. The increasing number of farm women's gatherings and the 1994 International Farm Women's Conference suggest that farm women are beginning to flex their political muscles. They may yet form a strong lobby group of their own.

POWER IN THE COMMUNITY

Outside agripolitics, within rural communities themselves, the authority and influence enjoyed by farming families have been notable. Yet, this authority is usually organised along gender lines.

Women tend to be excluded from the public sphere of power and influence because of their ideological association with the family and because of their responsibilities within the household. Middle-aged male farmers, on the other hand, have enjoyed a great deal of power and authority in smaller local government areas reliant on agricultural industries.[5] As a result, they have been able to influence the values of others and shape the course of events to suit their interests. Their authority derives from their access to, and control of, economic resources, from the dependence of the community on their economic activity, from the status accorded to them and from the strength of rural ideology. Their control of resources — in particular, land — is seen as important by the rest of the community, many of whom aspire to land ownership. 'There is no question that in the rural ideology ownership of land underscores the social worth of men as well as affording them economic and hence political advantage.'[6]

While land-owning men enjoy a great deal of respect in rural communities, many women report being made to feel secondary by professionals and others off the farm with whom they have to conduct farm business. The way women are viewed in rural communities can be demonstrated, for example, from the number of women who report that men ringing the farm on business matters will almost invariably ask to speak to their husbands. Many women, although not all, find this very offensive. Various words used by the women to describe how this makes them feel include 'cross', 'angry', 'irate', 'upset', 'amused at their ignorance', 'annoyed' and 'amazed'. This evidence of the negation of women's legal rights is widespread and finds support in the ideology surrounding the business of farming. As one woman noted: 'I have trained them that they will be happy to do business with me as I am the person who is answering the phone ... I have had to be assertive, especially with the accountant and perhaps two others, but especially the accountant who was initially not prepared to be dealing with the female partner of the farm.' For women who take charge of the books and run an enterprise, this can be particularly irksome. Judy controls the books in her partnership and makes all the arrangements for her husband's trucking business, an offshoot of their farm business.

That is a real bone of contention with me … you get your real chauvinists and they won't deal with me … And I have said to them, "Well, look, he is not going to be home for two or three days, if you want this load you are going to have to talk to me." "Oh, no, it's alright, I will talk to [your husband] when he gets home." And then [my husband] … when he comes home, he just sort of speaks to them and then turns around to me, "Well, can I fit it in?"

Kerry controls her own beef cattle enterprise while her husband takes charge of the sheep.

I had one guy the other day … ringing long-distance and he rang about three times each time asking for [my husband]. And it turned out that what he wanted to do was to collect semen from a bull, and when he did eventually get on to [my husband], [my husband] just said, "Well, it's Kerry you want", and handed him back … He could have saved himself a lot of trouble by just telling me what it was all about to start with.

Some professionals off the farm convey the attitude that women are not credible partners or lack knowledge about their industry; this irks many women and shows the strength of the assumptions surrounding farming and the roles of women within agriculture. Overall, women are still treated poorly by those they come in contact with in their dealings on behalf of the enterprise. Despite their legal status, the amount of work they do or even their knowledge of the farm's financial status, far too many women report being disregarded and ignored by professionals.

SUMMARY

The power of farm women is circumscribed. Their position as farm wife restricts their influence to a narrow domestic sphere. While their work within the enterprise and off the farm allow them a great deal of personal satisfaction and influence within the family, their power is limited. Despite the fact that many women report being involved, their influence on farm production decisions is minimal, because final decisions usually rest with male members of the family. Outside the family, the authority of farm women is negligible because of the ideological assessment of women and their position in the farm family. They have little involvement in traditional farm organisations or on local government bodies either because of their own traditional view of their role, lack of time because of family and household commitments or because of their feeling of being marginalised within the farm production unit.

The limited involvement of women in agripolitics should be cause for great concern among the farming lobby. Neglecting the opinions and energy of half the farming population is counterproductive when that half may be more educated and have a more intimate knowledge of the financial affairs of the family farm enterprise. Yet, the involvement of women is not being facilitated by these organisations, and women will remain constrained from involvement in agripolitics while they shoulder the burden of family responsibilities, and because of their lack of time and resources, their on and off-farm work and their own feelings of alienation because of partnership arrangements or because of the patriarchal structure of such organisations. Nothing will change unless the organisations make it easier and more acceptable for women to be involved. In the meantime, a women's farm organisation could tap a great deal of unused energy and enthusiasm. It is hoped that the emerging farm women's networks in New South Wales and Victoria will expand and meet this role so that women will be able to address their own concerns and add their voice to the public forum.

The following stories are included to illustrate the different experiences farm women have in gaining representation on agricultural organisations. Kathleen has been widowed for many years and was viewed by her community as a legitimate farmer. Kerry, on the other hand, farms with her husband and finds it difficult to achieve credibility in the public sphere.

Kathleen's Story

Kathleen's story was detailed in Chapter 4. Kathleen was widowed as a young woman and remembers taking control of the farm over the course of a harrowing week. During the time she farmed alone and before her son took over, Kathleen became an active member of the New South Wales Farmers' Association. While she did not involve herself in agripolitics while married, she subsequently took a keen interest in the farmers' organisation. She is accepted at local meetings where she has been the only woman to attend consistently for 23 years. On a number of occasions, Kathleen has represented the local group as a delegate at State conferences. Kathleen is given community support and approval because of her status as a farmer.

Kerry's Story

Kerry is 36, married with two children. She and her husband purchased their present 405-hectare grazing property ten years ago, and they have no legal association with any of their extended family. Because of this, Kerry has always gained a great deal of satisfaction from her own and her husband's efforts to build up the farm. Kerry feels she and her husband contribute an equal amount of labour on the farm. She runs the cattle enterprise; he, the sheep; she does raking and ploughing, he does baling and sowing. Despite her obvious knowledge and contribution to farm labour, Kerry says she is 99 per cent responsible for household tasks and childcare. Up until the time she had her last child, she had a substantial vegetable garden producing everything except for potatoes. Kerry describes her farmwork as her leisure because it frees her from her responsibilities in the home and because she enjoys this work so much. She finds time to attend the P and C and school activities, and involves herself in the organisation of local community events. Although Kerry does not do any paid work off the farm, she worked full-time for a year in a local factory during the first year of her marriage, a job she described as ghastly, in order to save enough money for a stud bull.

Decision-making is shared in their household because of the equal amount of time each partner spends on farmwork, and Kerry has no problem identifying herself as a farmer. The downturn in agricultural returns has made life more difficult for Kerry's family. She is aware that '… everything you do has really got to be making money. I just sort of feel I can't waste time … Farming expenses are so high. We spend so much on machinery maintenance that I often wonder if we are silly for not giving up farming.'

Her enormous contribution to her farm and family has not, however, led to her gaining representation on agricultural bodies, and yet, she would like to be involved in the cattle breeders' association. But as she notes:

I think if you are running a stud as well as you can, most guys don't get on those boards until they have got sons who are then looking after the stud. If you are doing all you can at home, you have got no time to be on boards and things. You are tired. But of course I am doing the kids as well ... Maybe if I was a man and just doing what I am doing so that I didn't have to do the kids and the house, I might feel quite differently. In fact, I think I probably would feel differently. But my involvement with the kids and the necessary things you have got to do in the house even if you don't want to just keep me too busy.

Kerry's busy lifestyle prevents her from taking an active part in her industry off the farm. She also senses that her contributions to agriculture and cattle breeding are not recognised in the wider community. Her valuable input is not sought by the organisations themselves. These organisations do not tap into the expertise of women in farming and, as a result, their experience is lost. As Kerry says, it is their loss. Yet, the failure to draw on the knowledge and experience of women farmers because of the patriarchal nature of the industry ensures that men control not only the resources of agriculture but also the knowledge. Traditional organisations have not allowed or admitted a female perspective.

CHAPTER 6

WORKING
FOR
LOVE

It's something we have to do. I mean, there's no great joy in housework, it's the bane of everyone's life.
38 year-old-farm woman, New South Wales.

C entral to the experience of work for farm women is the fact
that they usually take responsibility for all household labour.
Regardless of their age, stage of life, education or any other variable, farm women accept that they are primarily responsible for
housework. This chapter examines the nurturing role of women in
the household and in the community. In discussing the work
of farm women, it is important to note that not all women work
on the farm and not all work off the farm. The way a woman
chooses to allocate her time is influenced by a number of factors,
including the family structure and legal arrangement, the amount
of hired labour, her farm background, her availability, the economic circumstances, her education and number of children,
among other things.

WORKING IN THE HOME

W omen's compliance with the domestic role ensures that the
established sexual division of labour is legitimised and their relegation to the private sphere is effected. Yet, what farm women do

as part of their housework is diverse. Sometimes, farm families experience cycles of poverty brought about by drought, low commodity prices or fluctuating fortunes. During these times, women increase their work in subsistence production in an effort to save money. Many of the subsistence tasks performed by women as part of their housework can be seen to reduce costs and so make an economic contribution to the farm. They care for young animals, preserve produce, provide meals for workers and generally co-ordinate the farm. Yet, the pressures on farm women at the present time are forcing many to reconsider the way they allocate their time. Many report they are reducing their subsistence production as they move on and off the farm to work.

During my discussions with farm women, all stated they are almost totally accountable for the washing, ironing, cleaning and cooking and most reported being in charge of the garden. Fifty-three per cent grow vegetables, 71 per cent preserve produce, 58 per cent rear young animals regularly and 83 per cent have made clothes for their children. One-third make their own soft furnishings (curtains, cushions etc.) and several save money by cutting their children's hair. Sixty-four per cent of farm women also reported that they regularly provide meals for hired workers, usually shearers or casual labourers who are on the farm for short periods each year. Sometimes, the performance of this task can be extremely difficult. Kristen told the following story.

And the worst case was, which I still get annoyed about when I do think about is, [my second child] was something like about three months old, and I had my family over and the economy tank people … were erecting a tank … So for three nights I had three, sometimes four, extra men that I fed and provided accommodation for while my family were visiting us. So there were three of my family actually visiting and I had these three to four men for three nights while I had a new baby.

Sarah, a woman in her forties, who was involved in an inter-generational partnership with her husband and father-in-law early in her marriage, told a similar and perhaps more harrowing story of an incident which occurred during a shearing time.

I still remember … going out with a baby in the bassinet in the back of the car and a dog in the front of the car, and going around this mob of sheep and running round them with the dog. And then the dog cut them off — cut the sheep off at the gate, as they will do — and I just laid down on the ground and cried and cried. I thought, I just haven't got the strength or the energy. And we were in the middle of shearing. We had the wool classer staying in the house, I had to look after him — breakfast, lunch and evening meal. I was just exhausted. I was breastfeeding this new baby … so he was only three months old, and I had this extra man in the house to look after and I was also feeding the shearers. I had to get back and get the lunch on the table for all these men, and I lay down in the middle of the paddock and just cried … My father-in-law came and asked me [to get the sheep in] and I'm still angry to this day that he came down at 11 o'clock … and the lunch had to be on the table at 12 o'clock.

Despite the many pressures placed on women as a result of the various expectations, their acceptance of domestic labour underpins the shape of their lives. Yet, this acceptance is not without a great deal of irritation for many younger farm women. Louise, a 35-year-old farm woman, stated: 'No, no sometimes I feel you rage and rant about picking up, you know those sort of things, but no, look it's taken a while but I realise that he's just not going to do housework! He's just not! It doesn't matter what I do!'

Regardless of the feelings of aggravation expressed by many women about household work, their acceptance of responsibility in this area is evidenced by the fact that they often refer to the 'help' given to them with domestic tasks. Similarly, they may refer to their own farm work as 'help' to their husbands. Jane, a 29-year-old woman, explained how she does the lion's share of the cooking. 'Yes, I do. But my husband helps heaps. He has got to or else I wouldn't cope. If I have got to help him outside he has got to help me inside.' Many farm women indicate their acceptance of separate spheres with similar comments. Ruth, whose story was told in Chapter 3, commented that: 'Basically, we operate on old-fashioned inside the house then it's mine, outside the house then it's his.'

CHILDCARE

Women's almost total responsibility for housework extends to childcare tasks. Childcare is, in fact, seen as part of the private sphere of women, and the allocation of this work acts to confine and restrict women's activities in other areas such as farm work, off-farm work, community, social and leisure activities. The following table indicates the way childcare tasks are divided on the farms investigated in southern New South Wales.

CHILDCARE TASKS

Task	Women	Shared and/or hard labour
Childcare	54	9
Transporting children	53	10
Help with homework	52	11
Reading to children	53	10
Taking children to doctor dentist and for haircuts	56	7

JUGGLING TASKS

Responsibility for domestic labour and childcare, and the increasing expectation that they will work on and off the farm, is placing pressure on many women as they attempt to juggle disparate tasks. Because women accept that they will perform traditional female tasks, they report feeling guilty if all expectations are not met. For instance, Marianne, a 42-year-old farm woman who had been working off the farm for three years, reported feeling guilty that she was not keeping up the same level of task performance in the house: '... I don't leave a lot of lunch for him, so he generally has to hunt around for his lunch, which used to worry me as I didn't have it left ready for him ... But just lately, when I have been working four days a week, I found that I got a bit disorganised and haven't always had something for lunch. He has to hunt around for it.' Marianne's traditional beliefs and her own interpretations of her role on the farm are causing her to worry that she is not performing domestic chores as before, despite her obvious contribution in off-farm income.

While it is evident that married women are engaged in many areas of work, the challenges facing widowed and single women on farms are worth noting. They, too, view themselves as accountable for traditional female tasks as well as the outside farmwork. The problems this can cause are illustrated in the following quote from Deborah when she speaks about providing meals for shearers.

... it is dreadful work, see. Yes, the first year ... the locals were shearing and whatever, and I did it for the first year [provided meals], and I just thought I got no thanks for it and I was a fool because I had all the sheep work to do and the lot — and feed them, and see, I found I was getting to bed at two or three in the morning to get up at five and it just wasn't ... and you got no concession for price or anything else, so I decided to ... not do it. I was only a fool.

Age is a factor in the way women interpret their role on the farm. Most women over 40 years of age accept a traditional assignment of roles and are prepared to maintain their work in the household. June, a 64-year-old woman, commented that there was no dispute about who should take control of housework. 'No ... That's what I've been put on this Earth I suppose to do.' Myra, a retired farm woman, concurred with this view. 'No, because in those days you accepted your lot and you never expected your husband to do anything like that.' Despite the fact that many older women accepted a traditional assignment of roles in their own lives, they are aware that the world is changing and that sex roles are less stereotyped. Hannah, a retired farm woman, compared her own life on the farm with that of her daughter-in-law, Louise, who now lives in Hannah's old home.

Well, that's a big change now ... On the days Louise is teaching, [my son] would have [the baby] with him all the time and he would probably be quicker at changing a baby's nappy than I would be these days ... You know it has changed completely ... Oh, I think it is a good idea. Well, it doesn't do the men any harm. Besides, I think it suits that relationship between the father and the children ... Some of the farm wives have got their jobs to do outside too, so it is just fair that the men do a few in the house.

While Louise's husband shares the load, many others do not. Younger women find it more difficult to accept the expectations of their partners and their communities that they will continue to do all the domestic labour on the farm. They are now working in many areas and have seen no accommodating shifts from their husbands. Judy, a young farm woman, noted:

... occasionally, I get cranky because, if I've worked, the day that I work, I come home, and he's worked too, but he always, he doesn't understand that I'm tired. He'll want me to still run around and do it. It depends on how tired he is, you know, sometimes he'll get in and give me a hand. But other times "No, I've had a hard day", and sit down. And you keep, you do the work ... Occasionally, we have a few arguments where I say, "Listen here, mate! I've worked too today!"

Beth expressed similar sentiments. 'Since I have been working full-time, I would rather he helped more in the house — or I would rather he *did* more in the house, not helped — and that has been a source of irritation and frustration for me. I think he feels that I work but that is my choice and that is fine.' What is also interesting is that some women in their fifties are expressing these sentiments as they also are taking up diverse roles. For example, Carol expressed it this way: 'I suppose I maybe would get a little bit niggly if we really have had a full day outside, and I have been outside, and come in and then, I am just, the food is not quite on the table ...' Vicky, also in her fifties, found the assumptions unreasonable:

Yes, there is only my husband and I at home, but I am totally responsible even if I have been out helping in the yards all morning and come home. I find that they sit down and watch while I get the lunch ... I am used to it now, I think it is unnecessary, but I think, you know, it is an in-built thing in men — they just allocate you that as being your priority, and sometimes they make little concessions but mainly that's your field ... they forget you are tired too, that you've been out all morning.

Women are becoming more grudging in their acceptance of an assigned domestic role. They are now coping with a multiplicity of tasks both on and off the farm but are still expected to take charge of everything 'inside the farmhouse fence'. There has been little compensatory shift in the allocation of domestic responsibilities on the farm, because men seem to accept an ideology of wifehood which naturalises and legitimises the assignment to women of such tasks. The result for women is an increasing burden of work as they struggle to meet all expectations. Younger women on farms no longer accept the notion that women are somehow naturally better at housework. In fact, many women become extremely agitated and angry when such a suggestion is made. Gail, for example, said, 'No, that is a myth. That's an absolute myth! Of course they are not!' Kerry, whose story was detailed at the end of Chapter 5, notes more laconically, 'Housework doesn't require a great deal of anything except persistence!' Yet, despite their exasperation with the role prescribed for them, women do comply. The socialisation of men, societal beliefs, the labour allocation on the farm, their secondary place in the family and their lack of power inevitably lead women to taking a domestic role, despite their feelings of dissatisfaction and the stress of their other workloads.

WORKING IN THE COMMUNITY

T he nurturing role of women extends into the communities in which they live. They have always been heavily involved in the business of keeping their communities functioning at a level that ensures an adequate quality of life for rural dwellers. Older women have devoted much time and energy to voluntary community work throughout their lives. Younger women report that it is becoming more difficult to make the same commitment because of a lack of time and problems of distance. Increasingly drawn into farmwork and off-farmwork, they are having to curtail their efforts in the community. Economic pressures and the need for financial restraint are also leading many to question the devotion of precious resources such as petrol and wear and tear on the car to voluntary community effort.

Yet, women are still devoting a great deal of time to charitable works, community groups, their churches and their schools. They are members of organisations such as the Red Cross, the Country Women's Association (CWA), Meals-on-Wheels, show societies, hall committees, the Nursing Mothers' Association and the View Club, to name a few. Their efforts ensure that the community has adequate aged care, educational activities, charitable organisations and sporting facilities.

Women's voluntary involvement in education includes attending P and C meetings and, in some cases, school boards, helping at the tuckshop, cooking for the tuckshop, spending time in the classroom listening to children's reading or helping with story writing, providing transport for excursions, cleaning the preschool, sewing and cooking for street stalls and fêtes and sometimes, teaching scripture. However, women who work off the farm report that they face conflicts when attempting to perform voluntary work as well. Anna, a young farm woman with four children, noted:

> ... that's why I pulled out of tuckshop because every time I was on tuckshop I got rung up to see if I would do a casual day teaching and I wouldn't, and it was a very expensive day that I volunteered for tuckshop ... So I decided this year that, also we live a long way out of town and with the economic situation, I've just decided to cut petrol costs a bit ...

Chris, another young farm woman, echoed these sentiments when she explained that she had pulled out of reading at school because of her commitments to off-farm work and '... the expense of driving the car into town just for an hour. We thought the economics of it, it just wasn't worth it.'

The women who are not working off the farm sometimes have to cope with the problem of filling in the gaps for the working mothers. The friction created by some women withdrawing their voluntary services was referred to by Bernadette: 'Well, I go and listen to kids [read] while their mothers are merrily out working and that sometimes grates a bit.'

Women in rural areas invest a great deal of time facilitating the sporting life of their communities. Ken Dempsey states: 'Women [in rural communities] are expected to use their domestic skills to facilitate men's leisure and to be present to cheer men on in their pursuit of personal glory and public esteem.'[1] Several women surveyed reported being on the executive of the local football club, in the ladies' auxiliary and working in the kiosk on football days. They work hard to facilitate their children's sporting activities as well, driving them long distances to sporting events, sometimes coaching teams and working in kiosks.

Rural dwellers often combine their need for social activities with their greater need to hold fund-raising functions in support of community resources. Many women in rural areas not only attend these functions but also organise and cater for them. Claire noted 'If there is something on like that we usually go, and quite often you feel obligated to go because it is usually some sort of fund-raising ... It might be to raise money for the hall or it might be to raise money for the Red Cross or whatever it is. So you ... feel a bit obligated to go to those sort of things.'

The social and community life of rural dwellers, particularly in more isolated areas, is heavily dependent on the input of women. They are involved in planning and organising events, catering for them and cleaning up afterwards. There are few opportunities for women in more isolated areas to go out to dinner or attend the theatre, and financial constraints and tiredness often prevent them from pursuing this option regularly. Nevertheless, the work of women in their communities has been referred to as 'this work [which] produces the networks which make up the women's infra-structure of mutual aid so necessary to the survival of the com-munity'.[2] Because the community efforts of farm women are being curtailed, services essential to rural town survival are now in danger of closing down.

SUMMARY

T he degree to which women's identities are linked to the ideol-ogy of wifehood and motherhood leads them to accept a division of labour by sex, despite the conflicts which arise between their work in the home and their other labour. Women consent to their work in the home and do not challenge the gender roles because of the threat to their primary relationships. Yet, Sarah Whatmore describes the problems which arise for women as a result of not challenging such roles.

Such tensions reflect a fundamental contradiction in women's experi-ence as "wives" between their place in the "collective identity" of the family farm and their sense of identity as *individuals*. Significantly, in all cases of conflict arising from women's multiple labour roles, these conflicts are seen to be "women's problems", to be resolved by women adjusting their work-load. Most usually this means giving up, or reducing, those labour activities which compromise their primary duties as wife and mother. A redivision of domestic labour within the overall farm labour process, in such a way that men give up their privileged position with regard to household servicing work, is not considered.[3]

For women on farms, this means that everything they do is added to their primary role in the household. As they change their work patterns away from the house, their primary responsibility in the home can lead to dissatisfaction and irritation.

Nevertheless, what women do as part of their domestic role includes many tasks that add value to their enterprise or save on consumption costs. Many women keep an extensive vegetable garden, rear young animals, feed workers, make clothes and furnishings and cut their family's hair. Despite the obvious value of these tasks, women have not been credited with contributing to the economy of the farm with their domestic labour and their efforts are rarely viewed as real 'work'. Rather women's domestic labour is viewed as 'a role intrinsic to women's gender identity'.[4]

The nurturing role of women extends into their communities. Many give hours of voluntary work to ensure an improved quality of life in the country. Mona's story is included as evidence of the commitment of many rural women.

Mona's Story

Mona is 65 years old, married with five grown children. She has been on the farm for 46 years with her husband. When she first moved to the farm, they lived in an old house without electricity for several years. They have always grown crops and run sheep and cattle. Her husband owns the farm, and Mona, her husband and only son are in partnership in the business. Mona has always been responsible for all the work in the household and took charge of rearing the children. She has always kept a vegetable garden and milked cows for many years when the children were small. She separated the milk and made butter for the household. She has always had poultry and her own eggs and is currently rearing meat birds to supplement the farm income. For three weeks a year during shearing time, Mona provides meals for the nine workers involved.

Mona is heavily involved in the life of her community. She is currently president of the Catholic Women's League, treasurer of the football club, treasurer of the tennis club, works in the kiosk on football days, is on the volunteer roster to supervise the local swimming pool, is a long-serving member of the Red Cross and

CWA, works in the luncheon pavilion at the local show, and once a month, works for Meals-on-Wheels. When the children were at school, Mona spent many hours at the schools her children attended. Her commitment to providing services to her small community is extraordinary.

Despite her age, Mona has been working off the farm as a casual employee in two local post offices within 20 kilometres of her home. Because these are one-person operations, she fills in when the regular employee is on holidays or ill. Her income is spent on household items. On the farm, Mona helps out with the stockwork and is responsible for the bookkeeping; yet, she has no say in farm decisions.

The deterioration in farm commodity prices has had serious implications for her family. Their income has been drastically reduced and Mona has serious concerns about the effects on her husband's health. Mona's son has now moved off the farm to take full-time work. Consequently, the farmwork is being done pre-dominantly by Mona's 70-year-old husband. Despite their lack of income, they have not been able to retire from farming because they have been assessed as having assets above the set limit. As a result, Mona and her husband cannot get the aged pension. They have had their farm on the market for three years but have had no buyer express interest. Mona and her husband face the pressure of having to continue farming into their old age in order to secure an income. Mona intends to keep her job off the farm for the same reason. Life is very difficult for old people on farms who cannot access social security. That she and her husband cannot now retire from their farmwork with dignity suggests that there is a serious anomaly in the Australian welfare system. Yet, Mona's story demonstrates the enormous amount of work women have con-tributed to their communities to ensure the lives of rural dwellers are enhanced.

CHAPTER 7

WORKING ON THE LAND

> I always say if I'm ever going to get divorced it will be on a
> Wednesday afternoon after we've been drafting sheep! I'll walk down
> and keep going! ... It's annoying when you give your time and you're
> still [accused of] standing in the wrong place! I mean, I've talked to
> other farmers' wives, and they all seem to stand in the wrong place!
> *37-year-old New South Wales farm woman.*

A s economic conditions deteriorate, labour on farms is increasingly being provided by family members. As a consequence, farm women have taken on a more prominent role in the agricultural workforce. In fact, it is only on larger farms which are able to employ labour that women have the option of retreating from farm tasks. In Australia, where farm families have experienced a particularly severe downturn in commodity returns, farm women's labour is particularly crucial to the survival of their enterprises. However, because men take charge of the farm labour process, the farmwork of women is generally responsive rather than self-determined. That is, they are seen to be available to help when needed and are often called out with little or no notice. Gloria, an older farm woman, noted: 'Yes, when my husband needed help in the paddock, you would have to drop everything and go out and help.'

Men's control of farm labour stems from their ownership of land and the resources of agriculture. Because women usually enter farming through marriage, they may spend their lives work-ing on land over which they have no legal claim. Within the farm family, farming tasks are seen as more important than any other work on the farm because of the obvious link with income. As a result, all participants see the 'hands-on' jobs as the primary farm tasks, and women's work in tasks peripheral to production are often discounted, despite the fact women are making an economic contribution to the farm with such peripheral work.

WOMEN'S INVOLVEMENT ON THE FARM

The amount of physical farm labour undertaken by women is influenced not only by the presence or absence of hired labour but also by the availability of women, their legal status in the enter-prise and their background in farming. The trend to employ less labour because of a lack of financial viability sees women doing more farmwork. Lucy, a 29-year-old woman with four children under eight, discussed the decision she and her husband had taken to do away with casual labour. 'I used to work on the farm only when necessary simply because the kids were little … But this year, we decided … that I am going to have to help as much as I possibly can. Whereas we may have employed somebody from outside to help — well, then I will pitch in and help.'

Carol reported that, like many others, they had reduced their shearing costs by doing away with shed hands. '… at the last crutching we [sister-in-law and self] were both shed hands because we didn't employ anybody. We only employed the shear-ers. We cut right out on the shed hands and I think we are doing that again for shearing this year.'

The availability of women also affects their input to farming. The increasing trend for women to work off the farm may make them unavailable for farmwork. Women whose off-farm work is part-time report that they juggle their efforts on and off the farm in order to maintain their involvement in farm work. Sharon, who works part-time in the local town, works it out this way. 'The times I worked full-time I made sure it was never harvest time or cropping time … and my one day at school, I suppose there were times when you would have to juggle around a little bit ... there were times I suppose that some of the [farm] jobs had to be thought about before the day or juggled around a bit.'

Sylvia, who worked from home, reported similar attempts to integrate all her work. '... I try and work around it. If [my husband] wants me to drive the tractor while he has a break, I will put off if I have a typing job, and I will do the typing job that night while he goes back on the tractor. If I am going to be helping with the sheep, I generally try and organise it so that the typing can be done at another date.'

Where women's off-farm work is more highly paid and critical to the family, accommodations are made to support their enhanced income-producing activity. These women often withdraw from much of their farming work.

Another factor which affects the amount of farmwork performed by women is their legal status in the farm. Women are more likely to be actively involved on the farm if they have a legal stake in the enterprise. Those whose farms are run by extended family networks may not participate at all. Chris stated: '... because we're in a situation of sharing labour between brothers, there's always plenty of labour, so I've never been asked [to help]!' If women have legal status and a background in farming, they invariably make a significant contribution to farm tasks. For those who have neither, like Jenny, whose story was detailed in Chapter 4, their involvement is minimal.

> ... Like I've never been allowed to drive the tractor. They've never taught me. It's something they always believed that you had to be brought up on a farm to actually do. Like there's too many things that can go wrong ... They've never taught me to drive a tractor — which I don't mind really. Because really with all the other things a wife has to do, tractor driving is not one of them ... You go home and then you got to ... the man sits down and the woman cooks the meal and then cleans the house and does the washing ... while they're sitting on their bum ...

PHYSICAL LABOUR

Women are reluctant to be involved with machinery. They lack the necessary skills to operate and maintain complex machines effectively. Yet, because of the reduction in hired labour, women are performing some of these tasks as a matter of necessity. Forty-five per cent of the farm women in my study reported that they do some machinery driving. There is, however, a gendered division in the way these tasks are accomplished. For example, many women are prepared to plough but none report that they drive the header; very few women are confident enough to sow a crop; many reported difficulty with lifting heavy bags of seed or with understanding new types of air seeders; no women reported that they spray crops; some will rake hay but few will bale it. It appears that while women are increasing their work in this area, they are taking a secondary role and perform less critical tasks. Jean, a 58-year-old married woman, who works on the farm all day, put it this way. 'I don't touch the header or the windrower. I don't do any of the chemical sprays because that is beyond my capabilities any-how … I'm not confident enough to do it. I don't know enough about it. I used to do it before I was married when I worked with my father, but machinery has changed so much.'

Other women note that their already-busy schedule and lack of time prevent them from being involved in machinery driving. As Kristen explains:

Well, I don't like it for a start. It is not work I choose to do. I think that the business should make enough money that if we need extra people for driving, and I know that once I start doing it, I will be expected to do every-thing inside the home and also start off slowly filling in the role outside. Virtually be working up to part-time or full-time outside as well as what I have got to do with the children's school and home. I can't do it! I won't do it!

Women are far more likely to be involved in animal husbandry. Their involvement ranges from very occasional help to total responsibility for livestock management. For instance, one woman I spoke with has total control of a 100-sow piggery. Rhonda and Kerry, whose stories were told earlier in this book, are in charge of the cattle enterprise on their farms while their husbands look after the sheep. Two other women interviewed are responsible for the sheep enterprise, and two work and train horses. These women include among their tasks teaching stock to lead in preparation for shows, trimming feet, weighing and recording details. In all, 90 per cent of women report being involved in stockwork in some way — 47 per cent of these in a significant way, while 11 per cent have their own enterprises. Significantly, many women who work off the farm still work with livestock, although several mentioned their work in this area is necessarily reduced. Robin explained, 'I don't mind helping with the sheep work, but because I'm working off farm, I don't have much time to do it. But I might shift stock. That's about the extent of it or help in the yards with drafting and things like that. But it's not very often because I'm just not there.'

Other women who work off the farm report fitting tasks around their work commitments. Claire, who works an evening shift at a nursing home four nights a week, described her input into live-stock tasks as equal with that of her husband. 'When we are shear-ing, I work in the shed till three o'clock, have a shower, get changed and go to work.' (Note: shearing hours begin at 7.30 a.m.)

For the women whose farms are run by extended family mem-bers, their contribution to farmwork, including livestock tasks, is often not as great as they would like it to be. Chris expressed her discontent at her situation: 'If I'm needed, I just love it. But you sort of go along and they will try and find something for me to do so I don't feel as though I'm just standing, I think that is a waste of time.'

A constant concern for young mothers who are engaged in farmwork is the problem of child safety. Farms are one of the most hazardous of workplaces, and women working on farms with chil-dren must be constantly vigilant. Louise noted: 'The only time they've ever had any stitches or anything, always it's been up at the shed, and that's awful because you feel if I'd been at home with them instead of out there working they wouldn't have …' Significantly, many women expressed concern that they felt their husbands were less vigilant than themselves. For the women working off farm, many of whom leave very young children with their husbands, this can cause great anxiety. Michelle sums up the feelings of many young farm women: 'Yes, it worries me. I don't like them to go with [my husband] when he is working with machinery, because they get busy and forget about the kids and accidents can easily happen.'

Older women remember the care that needed to be taken to

protect children on farms. None of them reported experiencing the anxieties of many of the young women who leave their children behind when they go off farm to work. Dorothy, an older woman, remembered employing hired farm labour so that she could be relieved to look after the children at home. 'We were very careful ... [my husband] preferred to employ a man so that the children's safety would be in my hands. They wouldn't have to go with him, or he wouldn't have to take them.' Because of the changes in agriculture and the work of farm women, many of the younger women are not free to take this option.

TIME SPENT ON
PHYSICAL LABOUR

B ecause of the seasonal nature of farm labour, women find it difficult to determine the amount of time spent on physical farm tasks. When I asked women to estimate the amount of time they spent on physical labour, most had great difficulty doing any more than gauging the average amount of time, but stressed that there were times when they were engaged on a full-time basis and other times when there was little to do. The estimates ranged from very little time spent on farm activities to full-time all the time. For instance, Deborah, a woman farming alone, commented:

> The other morning, particularly, I left here at quarter to six with the idea that because it was hot that I would be finished by one. I would make myself finish. But because there were more flies to do and whatever, I didn't come back here until five. I mean, I had come back for a meal and drinks and whatever but it was quarter to five till five. Certainly in 19— when [my mother first passed away I was working from five in the morning till six all of that time when I was first left on my own.

Many older women estimate that at times they had spent 'one-third,' 'one half,' 'three-quarters' of their time or 'seven days' on farmwork. While not all the women were able to give any measure to the amount of time they spent, 7 of the 25 women under 40 who were interviewed estimated they did farmwork full-time; 8 of these women said 2 to 5 days a week and 5 estimated all morning every morning. Overall, 80 per cent of women under 40 are working on the farm from two days per week to full-time. Yet, several explained that the hours they spend on physical farmwork are reduced now that they work off farm.

FARM-RELATED TASKS

W omen undertake other types of farmwork which are not physically demanding but which, nevertheless, contribute directly to production. These include bookkeeping and 'go-fering' (errand-running). Bookkeeping on the farm remains a female-dominated task; far more women than men are in charge of the farm books. Furthermore, some women without any legal owner-ship status in their farms perform this task. In fact, 53 per cent of women are solely responsible for bookkeeping and a further 11 per cent share the task with their husbands. These results confirm those of studies done in other countries, all of which report farm bookkeeping to be a female-dominated task.[1] There is an obvious link here between the higher educational achievements of farm women compared to farm men and women's bookkeeping role. In my research group, 58 per cent of women had higher qualifications than their husbands, 25 per cent had equivalent qualifications and only 17 per cent were less well educated.

One of the other most female-dominated tasks on the farm is the 'go-fer' role. Women spend considerable amounts of time running errands and going off the farm for urgently needed parts or farm supplies. Most women see this as part of their role as 'farm wife'. Only one of the 64 farm women interviewed claimed they did no errand-running at all, while 84 per cent reported that they did a significant amount. For example, Cheryl, married 12 years, when asked how much time she spends on this task, replied:

> An enormous amount of time ... I think [my husband] sits there and thinks of things for me to do when he knows I'm going to town — probably I've been to town twice since we've been married where I haven't had to do something for [my husband] when I've been in there. There's always something to be done. In fact, [my husband] very seldom goes to town ... I usually do most of his running around in town.

Rosie described harvest time:

... you might have to drive to [a town 200 kilometres away]. I did a couple of times because they were in a hurry for something, so I'd race down there and get whatever they would want. Or I might race to [a town 50 kilometres away] or [a town 45 kilometres away] if they didn't have the part in [the local town], which nine times out of ten they didn't have.

Working off farm does not always limit women's involvement in this particular farm task, and many explained how they were often telephoned at work to take care of jobs in town. For example, Gail said: 'Oh no, it can be anytime, even at work. [My husband] will often phone me, "Can you call at so-and-so's on the way home" or "I will get so-and-so to drop something in to you", or I have often got to drop parts on the way to work and pick them up on the way home.'

Women in predominantly cropping areas describe how they need to be available at short notice to go for parts and other supplies. Michelle lives on a large farm in the grain belt of southern New South Wales. She described her experiences with errand-running. 'Yes, I usually get called upon the radio: "Fly into [local town] and pick up bits or drench" or "go to [town 100 kilometres away] if they haven't got it in [local town]". Or "Could you come and take a sample of grain to the silo". I usually get a lot of running around.' Kim, in the same area, reported: 'It's nothing for me to have to go into [town 80 kilometres away] three times in the one day.' Jenny, who runs her own small business full-time, still performs a great deal of running around. 'Actually, at harvest time after the lunch rush here, I'd leave the person here and ... I'd cook something here and run it out to them ... I come in handy at harvest time. I come in handy.' Farm women report that they need to be available and on call especially during the times of busy seasonal activity, regardless of their other work.

REWARD FOR EFFORT

D espite their efforts to ensure viability, many farm women are not receiving an adequate income from the farm. Thirty-three per cent of the women surveyed stated that there was no surplus from the farm and that any money went straight to the bank. Significantly more women in the cropping areas were in this position. For example, Robin described their farm income. 'It's definitely not adequate to live on this year and we will be relying on the family allowance supplement again ... and I may even have to look at getting extra work later in the year ...'

Those women whose husbands are involved in inter- and intragenerational partnerships often receive a wage from the farm partnership. This wage is usually based not on what the family needs to live on, but what the farm can afford to pay. This often leads to very real hardship. Chris explained their circumstances. 'We just all sit around and have a look at where we can cut costs and things like this, which at the moment [means] ... what we all think we can survive on ... The bank is virtually paying our wage now.' A large minority of families draw nothing at all from their farms. Instead, they live on the farm woman's wages. Several report that there is simply no farm income to share. It is evident that, despite the hard work of many farm families, very often there are no rewards for their efforts.

SUMMARY

W omen's involvement in farm labour is dependent on the amount of hired labour, their availability, their legal status and their farm background. Their involvement in physical farm labour is more likely to be responsive than self-directed, because many women see their farm labour as 'help' to their husbands rather than a legitimate job of work. When they do contribute farm labour, it is more likely to be in livestock management tasks rather than those jobs requiring them to work with machinery. Yet, the reduction in the number of hired hands has seen women moving into this area. When they do drive machinery, a gendered division of labour sees women taking responsibility for the less critical tasks. They do, however, perform a great deal of work on the periphery of production. They run errands, help shift machinery and men, provide meals and generally facilitate the process of production. As well, women's higher levels of education compared to farm men has led them to take control of the bookkeeping on a majority of farms, and this occurs even on those farms where women have no legal status.

Working on the land

Women are making a very valuable contribution to the productive process on their farms. Yet, the downturn in commodity prices has resulted in a third of farms receiving no income for consumption costs. It is very often the wages of the farm women which enable the survival of these families. Frances's and Sharon's stories are included as examples of the amount of farmwork performed by women on Australian farms.

Frances's Story

Frances is a widow aged seventy-three. She had a couple of years of high-school education before leaving to help her parents on their farm. She married in her early twenties and moved with her husband to a new farm. During the next 20 years, Frances had five children and performed a traditional farm wife's role. She had an extensive vegetable garden and orchard, preserved 'hundreds and hundreds' of bottles of fruit and jams, milked a cow, made butter, reared poultry, split the wood for the stove, poddied calves and lambs, fed hired workers, taught her children by correspondence for a few years and made 'everything they wore'. She doesn't remember ever having a holiday in those years. Frances did not get electricity until 16 years after she was married; lack of water was also a serious problem. Her husband died 25 years ago, when three of her children were still at school. She immediately took over the running of her farm and has done so, very successfully, ever since. Since reaching her seventies, she has downgraded her operation considerably and now runs only sheep.

Frances has always been involved in voluntary organisations and charitable work. She was a member of the CWA for a number of years, and for the last 20 years, has worked voluntarily one day a week at an old people's home run by an order of nuns. She spends the day doing the ironing.

Frances has never worked off the farm although her husband did wool-classing work during their marriage. She remembers being at home by herself with a tiny baby, sometimes for the whole week without transport other than the horse and cart. She remembers one incident clearly:

With [my son] a baby, and I can remember one night being down there milking the cow and didn't notice there was anybody around because the noise in the bucket, and I looked up and there was a man standing beside me. We used to get a lot of swagmen in those days. But he looked awful, this man, he wasn't like an ordinary swagman — he had his head bandaged and he said, "Could I cut some wood for a bit of tucker?" And I said, "I don't want any wood cut, thanks, but I will give you something to eat." He walked down to some wattle trees that were down behind me and I watched him go down. It was just coming on dark, and I thought, "Oh, I am not going to stay the night here!" Nobody ever had a lock on the door in those·days, you couldn't lock this house, there was no lock. So I put the horse in the sulky and took the baby with me and we drove down to [my parents] to spend the night down there.

Frances has always worked out on the farm, usually with stock. She also recalls walking across the paddocks with baskets of food two or three times a day, sometimes walking 3 kilometres each way. She has never driven machinery, leaving that to her husband and later to her sons (who return regularly to help with such tasks). In the past, she has had cattle as well as sheep, looking after them, for the most part, by herself. Farming decisions were made solely by her husband until his death. She has been making them ever since in consultation with her sons. Interestingly, her sons have moved off to their own farms or businesses, and her daughters have married and moved away from the district. Although she identified herself as a housewife during her marriage, she has seen herself as a farmer and grazier ever since. Nevertheless, she views herself as conservative and sees women's place in agriculture as a 'backstop for their husbands'. It was evident that Frances has had a very satisfying life on the farm. Her story illustrates not only the hardship of life on the farm for some women, but also the ability of women to perform the hands-on farm tasks when necessary and to make a success of their business. Frances has been a very good farmer and her farm shows every evidence of loving care.

Sharon's Story

Sharon is 47 years old, married with three grown children. She lives with her husband on their 1215-hectare grain farm in southern New South Wales. Four generations of Sharon's family live and work on the farm: her father-in-law and mother-in-law, she and her husband, her son and daughter-in-law and their children.

Sharon's younger son was on the farm as well, but is now working as a mechanic in the town because the farm cannot support him. Sharon's parents-in-law are old but are unable to draw the aged pension because they are still involved in the partnership. This is an added burden on Sharon and her husband, who are providing income for four generations.

In her own home, Sharon has always been responsible for the domestic tasks associated with rearing a family and running a business. When her children were small, she kept a vegetable garden, milked a cow and kept poultry. She also remembers making nearly all their clothes. During shearing time, Sharon provides meals for nine workers. She now shares this task with her daughter-in-law. Sharon is heavily involved in the life of her community. She holds positions in the football club and the tennis club. When her children were at school, she gave many hours of voluntary service to P and C activities and the tuckshop.

Sharon has often worked off the farm. She was a casual shop assistant for many years, and also worked as a craft teacher at the local school for one day a week until made redundant. She would dearly love to continue her off-farm work, because her income allowed them 'a lot of extras you wouldn't have otherwise. We did a lot on the house, added to the house and bought things in the house, the lounge and things.' Realistically, she sees her chances of finding work as slim. Also, 'It's got to be something that's a bit flexible too, because I do a lot of outside work here. It's a bit hard to tie yourself up full-time all the time.'

Sharon has always been heavily involved in farmwork. She enjoys driving the tractors. At the last sowing time, she reports,

> I did most of the work on one of the tractors because there was spraying to do at the same time. [My elder son] was doing nearly all the sowing with the air seeder. [The younger son] seemed to be doing a little bit of mechanics and going and loading the truck ... and [my husband] was spraying most of the time, so I had the other tractor with either the scarifier or the harrows.

Sharon has never been frightened of machinery, and remembers driving tractors as a child. She feels that she has just got used to the tractors as they have got bigger and more sophisticated. However, she feels unable to drive the header or the air seeder

unless the men set it for her, because 'I haven't got into the technological bit of it'. She concedes that they are using a great deal
more chemicals than they used to. 'Now you seem to spray before
and you spray it during and you're spraying again after. You're
spraying for red-legged earth mite or black oats or broad-leaf
weeds or whatever. You're definitely using a lot more chemicals.'

Sharon also helps with the stockwork, although her elder son
has in some ways displaced her from this task. She does a lot of
errand-running for the farm, particularly during harvest time. Her
husband and her elder son make the decisions on Sharon's farm,
although she feels she has a chance to have her say. She has never
been very involved in the production decisions on the farm
because of the intergenerational nature of the family arrangement.
In recent times, Sharon and her family have diversified into other
crops, and have reduced the amount of labour they hire because
their income has dropped sharply. Their standard of living has
dropped, and Sharon feels the family members are all working
harder even than 12 months ago in an effort to maintain their
income.

CHAPTER 8

WORKING FOR MONEY

The present economic situation has probably put a lot more pressure on me, because I realise now that I do have to work. I don't have a choice now about working for the commitments we have already made, and because we are not going to have an income on the farm probably for the next two years. So that means, yes, I do have to work.
43-year-old New South Wales farm woman.

One of the strategies adopted by farming families attempting to remain economically viable or to maintain their lifestyle standards is for a member of the family to seek off-farm work. This provides the income needed for the family to remain in farming. While it has been noted elsewhere that off-farm work is becoming a way of life for farm families in the United States, my own research in southern New South Wales suggests that this is also the case in Australia.[1] Of the 64 families investigated, women worked off the farm in 31; and men, in 28 (in several cases, both were working off the farm). The decision as to which partner seeks off-farm employment appears to depend on a variety of factors, which include the number of young children, the availability of off-farm work, the amount of farmwork to be done and who is best able to do it. Husbands tend to work off farm when the farm is less developed and their off-farm earnings will be higher. Women are more likely to work off the farm if they have higher education, high earning potential, a babysitter for the children and job opportunities.

Women in rural areas are at a distinct disadvantage when seeking work away from the farm. There is a high level of labour-market segmentation in Australia, and women are confined to a narrow group of, usually, lower status positions. In rural communities, this is exacerbated by the fact that employment opportunites close to farming areas are hard to find. Women's work in rural areas is characterised by low pay and lack of security. Farm women are, on average, better educated than farm men, but they may, in fact, be worth less in the marketplace because of the lack of skilled work available, the segmentation of the labour market and the wage structure, which allocates higher salaries to male workers. Perhaps, more importantly, farm women are more constrained by their family responsibilities than urban women. The strong emphasis farm women place on these responsibilities, the greater normative constraints on working mothers, the fewer occupational opportunities, the lack of childcare and the fact that they are usually solely responsible for domestic activities — all these factors force women to fit employment around their obligations.

The adoption of off-farm work patterns by a family member may change the way labour is allocated within the enterprise. When men are employed away from the farm, women often take over a larger share of farmwork. When women work away, very little changes in the home, and they may still perform the same level of farm tasks.

OFF-FARM WORK

M y study of 64 farming women reveals the significance of off-farm work to the survival of families in farming. In fact, with the exception of those who had babies, those studying, those who were over 60 and those farming alone, all but one of the women were generating income or were actively seeking work. Of even greater significance are the figures for women under forty. Of the 25 questioned, all but five with very young babies and two who were studying were earning income away from the farm. These figures suggest that women are making a far more significant contribution to their enterprise with their off-farm income than has previously been acknowledged or accepted. The fact that women with very small children are working off-farm illustrates, firstly, that women are sometimes under pressure to produce income, and, secondly, that the social relations of production on farms are changing. These women retain responsibility for domestic work and a large majority of them gives a great deal of their time to farmwork.

The type of work family members are doing in rural areas varies enormously. For women, the most stable positions appear to be those related to education and nursing. Less secure are those positions in home care, shop assistant work, teacher's assistants, casual typing, census collecting and cosmetic selling. Men who work off the farm tend to be engaged in casual shearing and farm labouring and contracting with machinery and share farming. Their work is mostly seasonal and related to agriculture. Women's work is also characterised by its part-time nature. Fifty-eight per cent of the women interviewed work for less than 20 hours a week; 16 per cent for more than 20 hours and less than full-time and 26 per cent work full-time.

Predominantly, women work for less than 20 hours a week in jobs that have few benefits such as holiday and sick pay. As well, the lack of employment opportunities and the burden of other responsibilities lead many women to take jobs for which they are overqualified. In my study, 32 per cent of the working women report being overqualified for their off-farm positions and are, therefore, not working to the level of their ability and training. Being unable to find work for which one is qualified can be quite devastating for some women. For example, Judy, a young farm woman who had been brought up in a capital city and had two university degrees, reported: '... for the first time in my life, when I came down here, I wished I had done nursing or teaching or something like that ... which you could do in this area ... I am totally overqualified ... There is really no scope for my field here unless I could get a job at [a town 120 kilometres away], but that is still too far to travel every day to make it economically viable.' This highly qualified woman could see no opportunity to use her chosen skills in a farming community, and now faces the prospect of having to reassess her goals and perhaps retrain in teaching or nursing in order to find employment. Unfortunately, Judy is not the only woman interviewed with specialised skills and no opportunity to use them. The lack of opportunity for off-farm employment for women who wanted to work in the area of their training was the most difficult constraint many women faced.

Those who are working off the farm report that their reasons for taking a paid job are either personal, such as a need for enhanced self-esteem (39 per cent); financial necessity (35 per cent); or some combination of both (26 per cent). Vicky, a woman in her fifties, who works for economic reasons, explained, 'I work for money ... I have no career aspirations as far as work is concerned because I'm past that. I've done all that. I mean, I gave up my career when I came to the farm and I swore I would never work again. I thought I was going to come into this lovely ... situation and of course it's just never happened. So I personally work for money!'

Many women who gave personal reasons for working off farm concur with Robin, who said:

> Yes, when I started, it had nothing to do with finance, because as I said, it's only really paying childcare. It was to do with myself, my own reasons, yes, and to keep my mind doing something ... like self-esteem I suppose ... to do something. And also to be in the community rather than isolated on a farm. Not that you are that isolated — but mentally isolated.

Beth felt she was working for both personal and economic reasons:

> Well, initially, it was because I needed the stimulation. On the farm it is always, I am the farmer's wife, not the co-partner. Even though that doesn't necessarily follow through to my personal relationship. But that is certainly the perception, that you are only ever helping, and I really needed to do something for me that I felt that I was in control of and that I had something to contribute and that I did for myself — not as somebody's wife or somebody's mother ... So that probably the primary reason is for self-satisfaction and self-achievement although now ... The emphasis has changed and my income is pretty vital.

OBSTACLES FOR
WOMEN SEEKING WORK

T he main obstacles mentioned by women working away from the farm or looking for work include the lack of opportunities, lack of childcare and problems of distance. Lack of opportunity is a problem for Mary, a trained nurse who has tried to gain employment at four hospitals within a 100-kilometre radius of her home. Lack of jobs is a constant theme for rural women. Janet summed up the feelings of many when she said, 'Really [there's] nothing available. Not for an untrained, unskilled worker, unless I was prepared to go and clean houses. I can't clean my own so why am I going to go and clean somebody else's?' Cheryl, who had managed to find one and a half days' work as an assistant at the local school, stated: 'Unless you want to pick vegetables during the vegetable picking season or something you might be able to pick up a bit of that ... other than that, there would be very little around here. Probably none I would say.'

Lack of childcare was another major obstacle affecting many women. For example, Anna explained, '... I had an opportunity to do an eight-week block of teaching straight ... but there's just no one I could leave my child with for that length of time ... The young girls, they're either too young so that you can't use them or they're at school, or once they get of age, they leave the district.'

While childcare was the most often mentioned obstacle, distance to the city or the nearest town was cited by many as a major problem in seeking employment off the farm. For instance, June, trained in a specialised area, stated she would need to travel 65 kilometres to the nearest city to find work in her chosen field. With four young children, this was not an option she could consider on a regular basis. Nevertheless, she has her name down for relief work in the city. Anne reported the problems she encountered with distance and insecure employment conditions: 'I was working in Payless in [a town 40 kilometres away] packing shelves, but I found the travelling ... I was "on call" — casual ... and I found on the highway, it gets a bit nerve-racking driving that highway 25 miles [40 kilometres] morning and night during the busiest time.'

The part-time option taken up by many farm women leads to other problems for those seeking to carve out a career path. Marianne pointed out that she was forced to work four half-days instead of two full days, which would have saved her petrol and travelling time, because there was no flexibility at her place of work. Little accommodation is available for women travelling long distances for part-time work in rural areas, and certainly, no childcare provisions are available.

The lack of assistance for women working off the farm extends to their own families in many cases. Ten of the working women surveyed (32 per cent) felt they received some help from husbands to facilitate their jobs, and 21 (68 per cent) received none. Many, like Gwenda, felt their husbands were also under a great deal of pressure to increase their workloads on the farm. 'Well, before I started working full-time … he said, "Oh, that's all right, I will help around the house and I will do the washing and I will cook tea every night." But he didn't cook tea once. And it was not because he didn't mean to, but he was just so busy and things were on …' Many women agree that their husbands are busy and they therefore don't expect them to take on more, despite the fact that they themselves have done just that, often for economic reasons. Sue explained: 'Again, because of the casual nature of the work and because I don't think it is fair to expect him to come in from doing a lot of work outside to have to take on more inside.' However, some of the women were finding the pressures and expectations on themselves extraordinarily difficult. Louise is one of these:

> It's just becoming more and more demanding. Whereas he can't leave the farm and get a job elsewhere because someone has to run the farm, she can. So therefore it's just another thing that she has to do … But you know you've got to be there at the P and C, you've got to be there at the charity thing doing your bit and making sure you're putting your family's bit in. But it just seems to be becoming insurmountable!

THE EFFECT OF OFF-FARM WORK ON OTHER AREAS

Women's work off the farm inevitably affects all other areas of their lives. The amount of hours they work in paid employment is crucial to determining whether they will be available to work on the farm or in a voluntary capacity in the community. Women do try to continue their other obligations by working around their paid employment. Two of the women I spoke with work as night nurses so that they might maintain their work on the farm. Two others who work full-time employ hired labour in their small businesses so that they might continue to do their turn with Meals-on-Wheels and at the school. One woman who is now working full-time had devoted a great deal of time to community effort. She has now changed the way she contributes to her community.

> I am now financially supporting [these organisation] ... so instead of having me, they are getting a donation from me ... I help with Meals-on-Wheels and I am sort of a liaison officer for them, and I am also a connection for the medical centre in [the local town] ... There are a few of the older people who don't have phones on. So if the medical centre needs to contact them, they ring me. So, yes, there are a few things that I have still got my finger in.

The effect on women's farmwork is marked. Sixty-five per cent of women who work off the farm report that they have reduced their farmwork because of their unavailability. Beth was one of these. '... greatly, because I'm just not here. Before I went out to work full-time, I was probably out on the farm three days a week helping move sheep or drafting sheep.' Others, such as Vicky and Sue, reorganised their labour. Vicky: 'Yes, it's a bit of a problem. Like, I have to get up really early if [my husband] wants to drive sheep, or I have to do it when I come home in the afternoon.' Sue: 'It affects it in that my husband has to work around what I am doing. For instance, we are feeding sheep at the moment ... and we had to get up at 6 a.m. this morning to get the sheep fed ... so he has to work his day around in order to accommodate me ... I mean, if he wants me to help him, he has to organise his day around.'

Most working women report that the effects of off-farm work on their housework are dramatic. Many tasks in the home are simply left undone, and most women report that help from other family members is not to be relied upon. Comments from women included:

> Oh, I just don't do the housework. I do the basics — the washing, the cooking and clean the bathroom. The vacuum [cleaning] doesn't get done, the windows stay dirty …

> The four days I'm working I don't get that much done. Then on the days off I'm too tired to.

> I come home very tired and can't be bothered about housework. So what doesn't get done on the weekend just doesn't get done.

Off-farm work has had an effect on the health of many farm women. While 55 per cent of women claim there is no change in their sense of well-being, 16 per cent felt better for working away from the farm and 29 per cent felt their health was adversely affected. Robin described her improved outlook this way. 'Probably [off-farm work] has a positive effect in that I'm more conscious of myself and I probably keep myself more healthy. When I'm at home all the time I tend to — because I'm not happy, or not totally happy. I get slack about myself and put on weight and slob around the house. Yes, definitely not as happy.'

On the other hand, Maureen, now taking a break from off-farm work, described her experience.

> When I was working off-farm … I used to come home absolutely exhausted every day and then I would sometimes try and go up to the sheds and do a little bit up there. No, I was mentally exhausted, as well as physically exhausted I think. I would come home and I would sit down and I would not probably move for sometimes half an hour!

The stress experienced by some women who feel they have to work off the farm is a hidden result of agricultural restructuring and the economic crisis in rural areas. It is a factor which is not being addressed by the women themselves or the wider agricultural community.

SPENDING THE MONEY

D espite the pressures in other areas, women are bringing cash into their farms. Often, this money is critical to the survival of the family in farming. Significantly, 77 per cent of the working women surveyed spent their income on household expenses and less than a quarter used their income on themselves. These findings confirm that women are continuing the practice established by earlier generations of farm women of covering the family's consumption costs — women still feel responsible for the needs of the household. Whereas older women took care of this by producing subsistence goods and by conducting small enterprises, contemporary women are achieving the same end by taking paid employment. Beth explained: 'It is my money that buys the groceries, buys the clothes for the children and me and any other sort of incidental expenses, and if that wasn't there, then the money would have to come from the farm.' Janet also sees her income as critical. '... I like to work, I enjoy it, but also if I didn't, we wouldn't do anything for the house. The farm just doesn't extend itself down this far, which is probably typical of lots of farms ...'

LEISURE TIME

L eisure time is a scarce commodity for farm women. Yet, it appears from the comments of farm women that 'free time' is not a prerequisite for leisure. They tend to define leisure activities in unusual ways. For instance, six women described farmwork when asked about their leisure, and three mentioned voluntary community work. Several defined their own leisure in terms of their children's activities, so that, for example, taking children to their weekly sport is perceived as leisure for themselves.

Because farm women find pleasure in their work and work-related activities, this in turn enhances the family's quality of life. Nevertheless, a high 47 per cent of women report that they do not have enough leisure time at their disposal. Twelve per cent feel they could make time and 41 per cent feel they have enough. Women report that a lack of time and money prevents them from pursuing their own leisure. In fact, 16 per cent of women questioned revealed that they had recently withdrawn from a leisure activity because of financial pressures. Maria was one of these. 'Well, I was playing basketball last year but I gave that up because of the ... cost of petrol.' A lack of time brought about by the fact that she is now working full-time off the farm has caused Sarah to curtail her much-loved embroidery. 'Yes, I do miss that. I go to the cupboard where all the material and all the cottons are, and I think, "Oh yes, I'd love to do that again" ... but I realistically don't have time ... But I keep thinking that one day I'll get back to that cupboard and I'll bring all that out again and do it. I don't know when ...'

Both time and money constraints have made it difficult for Kristen and many others to give time to themselves. 'By the time that I get through all that I have got to do at the moment, two things prevent me. One is economic at the moment and the other is that there are just not enough hours in the day. Perhaps that is my fault for not actually giving it [my leisure] a priority. But with money so tight, it actually gets fairly well down the list.'

Many women are concerned that their husbands also have little quality leisure time — in fact, 63 per cent feel their husbands do not have enough time for leisure activities. With the retraction of hired labour and the pressure to work harder, men find it equally difficult to allow themselves adequate free time. Gwenda worries about her husband's lack of time to look after himself. 'He plays tennis but under sufferance. I mean, he loves it, but he has got so many other pressures that it is a hassle to get there. He enjoys it while he is there but when he gets home, he says "I should have done this" or "I should have stayed home!"'

Lack of leisure time for farm families extends to a lack of regular holiday time away from the farm. No women report that their family takes any more than two weeks a year in holidays and, in fact, 50 per cent report that they have no holidays at all.

We bought a tent many, many years ago ... actually, my parents bought it, and it has sort of just gradually become ours and it is rotting — it's tearing and rotting, but we still use it ... So we have very cheap holidays. We go somewhere where it is very cheap to pitch it and then we ... just walk around or go for a drive.

On an average we have a holiday ... every three, four years, I suppose. We were going to go after sowing ... we were supposed to go down to Victoria and look for a windrower, but I don't think we will now. Well, now there's too much to do all the time.

We try to get away — we had one week in January this year. We had two weeks last year. We usually try and get two weeks a year ... that's all the holidays we take. But this year we only had one week because harvesting was late and we had to get back for shearing so we only managed one week.

The last two years we have been lucky. We have got cousins in Sydney so we have gone and stayed with them for two weeks — which is still pretty hard when you are in a family situation and with other family members, you are not getting away by yourselves.

We usually slip away whenever we can just for a long weekend or something, but we can never leave here for more than a couple of days because of the stock.

Sometimes, I have gone for three years without going anywhere for a rest. In the early 1980s, my husband and I didn't leave the farm for six years.

… in eight years we have had, I think, four small holidays — a week or ten days, but not on a regular basis.

It's always only been up to Queensland to my mum's. We've never been able to afford a really great, whizzbang holiday. Never. It's only now we've got a newer secondhand car … Like money's always — it's never been there. I married the national debt!

We went on one two years ago and that was the first one we had been on in about ten years. No, you can't afford to go on a holiday.

We sort of don't go — you know a lot of people go to Batemans Bay the third week of January every year. I mean, we don't do anything like that! We went to Sydney for a week this year. We didn't go anywhere the year before and I think we went away the year before that.

We haven't had a holiday for a few years … The economic situation, we just can't afford it.

No. We haven't for years had a proper holiday since we used to go down the coast. We bought a tent — again, that was economical as we just couldn't keep affording to pay $600 a week down there for accommodation. So we bought a tent and we try to get away once a year. But it has been — the last couple of years — it has only been two or three days at a time and maybe twice a year. That's all. We haven't had a proper holiday for ages.

The concept of leisure as free time remains, for many farming families, elusive. Few such families ever experience the notion of a free weekend or four weeks' annual leave. The financial restraint created by the rural crisis in agriculture, and the resultant constant pressure of work for little reward, mean that the urban concept of leisure as free time is not easily experienced. Far too many women report that they and their husbands have not enough leisure time. Nonetheless, many of the women in the study define their own leisure in terms of pleasurable activities which could include farm-work, off-farm work, community work or childcare tasks. In fact, many women do not feel disadvantaged, because they feel their lives encompass many activities which give them and their families an enhanced quality of life.

SUMMARY

T he trend towards off-farm work as a strategy to remain viable is continuing on Australian farms — many men and women are supplementing the family income with work away from the farm. For women, finding work in rural areas can be a difficult proposition. Consequently, many end up taking lowly paid jobs which are part-time and lack security. Farm women experience problems with a lack of opportunity to pursue their careers, with the distances they must travel, with lack of childcare and with inflexible working conditions.

Highly significant is the number of women under 40 who work off the farm in some capacity. The pressure of their workloads is cause for real concern. Yet, it is often the women's off-farm wage which is keeping the family fed and clothed. All women are concerned about the increasing expectations being placed on farm women. Older women are more likely to see the problem in terms of the children of the family. Frances, for example, explained, 'I think they [younger women] have to make ends meet. I would prefer to see them stay home and rear a family but it is not always possible. So I think children miss out on a lot if their parents are away working.'

Younger women are more inclined to see the pressures in relation to the women themselves, and expressed concerns for the well-being of mothers. For example, Kristen stated eloquently:

Well, I wouldn't criticise them. A lot of the women I see working off farm, they work off farm and keep everything spick-and-span at home, bring in the money, get very little reward for it and are under a tremendous amount of pressure. I really admire a lot of them. I mean some of them do it for their sanity, but a lot of them that I know are doing it to actually just survive. To actually put food on the table and are doing it fairly quietly too.

While most women work off farm for financial reasons, many women go off the farm to work for personal reasons, which include a need to achieve in their own right. Often, the women note they are seen as a helper on the farm, and they suffer a lack of self-esteem in this situation. Many of the women involved in inter- or intragenerational partnerships feel unfulfilled and gain little satisfaction from the farmwork in which they are involved. The result is that women are looking off the farm for employment opportunities which will provide them with both personal satisfaction and, increasingly, the much-needed money to survive. However, the family and farm responsibilities that these women have make it very difficult for them to commit themselves to outside employment, which tends to be fitted around everything else they do. The fact that women enter farming through marriage also makes it difficult for them to plan their lives accordingly. Those women who had studied and trained in specialised areas before marriage, and now find themselves in an isolated farming community with no access to employment where their skills can be used, are completely unprepared for their current situation. Industries willing to relocate to isolated farming communities would have a ready pool of willing labour among farm women and their older children, many of whom must leave such communities to find employment. Regional development is a strategy governments should be encouraging as a matter of urgency.

Increasingly, women are seeking off-farm work to keep the family going, but the work that is available may be unsatisfactory. Those women who are working, particularly for more than 20 hours a week, reduce their input into farmwork. Many others report that jobs are reorganised around their availability. However, few women receive significant help from family members with household and family responsibilities to help them with their added commitments. While many women state that their husbands are also far too busy, there is a perception that domestic chores remain the responsibility of women. Yet, while many women report feeling better for working off the farm, a significant minority report stress-related symptoms which could affect their health.

The lack of quality leisure time for farming family members is evident from this study. While women often see their leisure as a state of mind and not as free time, evidence has shown that men and women on farms do not have enough leisure time. That no families have more than two weeks' break a year, and that half the families in this study have no break at all, is indicative of the tremendous financial pressure farming families are under.

Sarah's story demonstrates the pressures on some farm women to produce income to enable their families to remain in agriculture.

Sarah's Story

Sarah is 45 years old, married with two teenage children, a boy and a girl. She has nursing qualifications and is currently completing a tertiary degree. She has been married for 23 years, and is now a joint owner of her 485-hectare farm with her husband. They run sheep and grow cereal grain crops.

Sarah has been working off the farm for most of her married life. Three years ago, she took a full-time job because the farm had simply not been returning enough money to pay household expenses. As well as studying, Sarah is also responsible for all the household tasks and meals in the home, does the gardening, keeps poultry and takes responsibility for making sure the children are transported to their activities. Although she is too busy now, in the past, she reared young animals and made the children's clothes and some soft furnishings. Over the years, Sarah has contributed many hours of voluntary work in her community. She has always been involved in church activities, running stalls and catering at church functions, she has helped at the school, spending time at the tuckshop and on the Parents and Friends Association, and is a member of a craft group.

Although Sarah finds it difficult to work on the farm now because of lack of time, she was heavily involved in stockwork when the children were small. She still does some of the errand-running when she is in town for her off-farm work. Her involvement in farm decision-making is minimal despite her legal status in the enterprise. Sarah has little time for leisure, although she sees gardening as her leisure activity. She has, however, had to give up her beloved craftwork.

Sarah does not identify herself as a farmer, preferring to describe herself as a nurse. As she noted: 'I always had this feeling that when you marry into a farming family that the farm is there, it's his, even though I know that's not how my husband feels, but that it really doesn't belong to me.'

Sarah sees her son as a future inheritor of the farm, although she has insisted that he gain a tertiary qualification. She does, however, feel that her commitment to the farm is not what it once was. Although her husband is a member of the local farmers' organisation, Sarah has never joined and has no involvement in agripolitics. She does, nonetheless, identify strongly as a feminist. As she explained: 'If I see farm women in my work, I do get them to look at what's going on in their own farming organisations and where they're placed in that organisation and how much say they have in it, and that they do have a right to have a say.'

Sarah is a determined woman who has moved outside farming in order to seek autonomy. She identifies strongly with her off-farm occupation, and has an awareness of the patriarchal nature of farming that has operated to give her a secondary role on the farm. Despite her awareness and her workload, she still finds herself responsible for family and household work, and acknowledges that she has very little time for leisure. She has attempted to maintain some voluntary work in her community, although this has necessarily been reduced. Women like Sarah appear to be bearing the brunt of the economic crisis in agriculture because patriarchal gender relations operating on farms have not relieved them of their unpaid family work.

DOWN (AND OUT) ON THE FARM

> We really have to watch everything we buy, everything. And the kids are going without ... I find we always are forever saying no to the kids.
> *28-year-old New South Wales farm woman.*

Australian farm families are struggling to remain economically viable. Deteriorating terms of trade, increasing costs of inputs, low output prices and high interest rates are problems faced by all families involved in agriculture. The way these pressures impact on individual families is very much dependent on the size of the farm, regional variability, the commodities produced, the level of capitalisation, the level of indebtedness and the amount of off-farm income produced. For instance, families on mixed enterprise farms appear to be more sheltered from market fluctuations (because of the ability of the enterprise to spread the risk) than those in more marginal areas dependent on cereal-crop growing.[1] Likewise, those on larger farms report a greater stability than those on smaller farms. However, across most farm industries, families have had to cope with a reduced cash flow. In my research with women on farms in southern New South Wales, all but one of the 64 reported a serious downturn in income to their farms.

The economic changes in the last decade have acted to reduce the viability of farming families worldwide. Unlike their predecessors, who were not so exposed to the exigencies of a volatile marketplace, farming families today have to trade in global markets. Such exposure does not ensure a secure economic climate in which safe financial and management decisions can be made with any certainty. Meanwhile, the control of input and output prices by agribusiness concerns is increasing the marginality of family farming. Consequently, the last ten to 15 years have seen a considerable decline in the economic security of farming as an occupation, a decline which has impinged on all family members. Net farm incomes have fallen over the long haul as farms have become larger, more specialised and more dependent on fossil fuels and agribusiness technology. In fact, many farms have had to enlarge in order to produce more so that they cover increased costs of inputs and maintain existing profit margins. As Sarah Elbert states, it is a cruel irony that the mushrooming development of agribusiness appears to be killing agriculture.[2] Joanne explained how input costs impact on their income on the farm. 'Probably the income has gone up but then the overhead costs of everything have just doubled higher than what your income did, so actually you haven't made any more really.'

Spiralling costs are a problem for all farm families as agribusinesses increase their control of the marketplace and force farm families into an unfavourable cost–price squeeze. Sue, a young farm woman living in the wheat belt area of New South Wales, stated: 'Well, the last couple of years the price for your wheat [went down] and that's made a big difference — with interest and things — fuel and that going up all the time and then the price of your produce dropping like it did, that really shot our budget to pieces last year.' As many women explained, these increasing costs can sometimes leave the farm enterprise in a negative income situation. A very frustrated Chris, a farmer in the wheat-growing area, said: 'You put your wheat in silos and look at all the costs that go out — your handling charges. Here six months ago, we got a bill! A bill for our wheat!' Sylvia also lives on a wheat farm in New South Wales. She reported: 'There is just no farm income … At a rough guess [we got] $7000 in wheat payments last year and $15,000 in bills.'

Spiralling input costs are of recent origin. Many of the older women remembered that things were once different. Elsie, an older woman retired from her mixed enterprise farm, explained how things have changed. 'It didn't take as much to keep you going years ago as what it does now. Costs have skyrocketed. Yes, no comparison really.'

Thirty-three per cent of the women questioned are on farms where there is no surplus income for household expenses. Jenny explains it this way. 'The farm income I don't see as income. I mean, it is there to pay the interest and to pay that bill and pay that bill ... No, it is not our household income.' In fact, several of the women in the cropping areas reported that their bank had intervened to restrict their spending. Jane explained that they had twice had their accounts frozen by the bank. Intervention by her parents and the taking on of off-farm work by both Jane and her husband had eased the situation. Several women reported similar financial constraint. Janet, who lives with her family on a cropping farm and who is desperately seeking employment, put it this way:

> I would say that really the "pinch" is only just being felt now — say, in the last six months — and your coming now is opportune because it is only this week that we have sat our family down and said, "Things are desperate, so this is how you know things are going to be. We don't even spend 20 cents on a lolly without due consideration because that is how bad it is." So I would say that you would probably find that a lot of people are like that.

In summary, the economic changes affecting farm families as a result of the downturn in many commodity prices are low or negative incomes, coupled with spiralling costs and interest charges, and an increasing intervention and control by banks. In some cases, this had led to banks restricting access to credit and causing real hardship to families.

THE EFFECTS OF ECONOMIC CHANGES ON FARM FAMILIES

The effects on the families involved of these economic changes are extensive. They include the movement to off-farm work by many women and men in farming; an increase in time devoted to farmwork by men, women and children on farms; a decrease in the standard of living for farming families; an increase in reports of health stresses on family members; changes in commodities produced by many farm units and an increase in production; a decline in the amount of hired labour employed on farms; increasing difficulty being experienced by farm families in making informed production decisions as prices fluctuate markedly; and an increasing reliance on the family allowance supplement as one of the few forms of reliable, steady income for those households with children.

The taking of off-farm work by family members has been discussed in Chapter 8. That this has been a radical change in the division of labour on farms is evident from my research. Older women interviewed had experienced a very traditional division of labour. As Kathleen stated: 'It just wasn't done for farm wives to go to work … They just didn't do it. They were there to help their husbands.'

All but 9 per cent of the women questioned felt they and their husbands were working harder and longer for less reward than at any previous time. The remaining 9 per cent were older women who felt they and their husbands had worked just as hard 30 to 40 years ago, but agreed that now they were working for less than at any other time. The pressures of these increased workloads and reduced incomes rebound on all family members. As Janet explained: 'All the hours [my husband] spends he has been getting a lot less. And yes, the children have had to do a bit more work. I keep saying to them that it is going to have to increase all the more, and if I am fortunate enough to get a job, it definitely will.'

The increased workloads have led to other developments, including a lack of leisure time for family members and a need for some women to withdraw from voluntary community work. Such consequences have a damaging effect on the health of individuals as well as the 'health' of the rural communities of which they are a part. Older women are not immune from these increasing work pressures. As Vicky, a 56-year-old farm woman, noted:

> You know, I do feel that when you get to our age, there are a lot of things that we worked hard all our lives for and therefore that we should be entitled to … The family having gone and there are certain sorts of niceties that one feels entitled to, like enjoying that drink at 6 or 7 o'clock at night … there should be nice times during the day and we are working so hard that those nice times almost don't exist any more …

Over 90 per cent of farm women surveyed felt they had experienced a drop in their standard of living. This decrease in standards had occurred in several lifestyle areas. Many areas of restriction have been discussed in previous chapters, and a selection of responses is included here to highlight the effects on individual families.

I don't think I have bought new clothes for five years.

I don't want the Earth or whatever, but I really would like to be able to go and buy the groceries and shoes and a few extra activities for the children without actually finding that I can't get my hair cut ...

I would just like to be able to, if they needed something new, to be able to buy it, and we can't ... even little things we can't ... they have got an excursion coming up that I have known about for months, and it's not until the end of the year, and I have been saving up for it just so they can go on it.

I have really watched what I have bought ... I am fairly careful — no chips or junk food or anything like that because we couldn't afford them anyway ... But gee, sometimes I feel like a nice treat myself. I would love to have one in the cupboard sometimes ... ..'

The drop in the standard of living for farming families is a widespread and general trend in agriculture, resulting in an increase in anxiety and stress levels amongst the farming families interviewed. The increase in stress-related symptoms among the women employed off the farm was noted in Chapter 8. Several women also reported that the effects of long, hard work for little return, coupled with financial problems, were creating stress-related problems for their husbands. For example, Vicky reported: 'I have seen my husband age in the last 15 months like I couldn't believe ... I have never seen him as stressed ... for the first time we are in a debt situation, which, at our age, is really frightening. How we are actually going to pay back the debt ...' Other women interviewed expressed concern that their husbands had withdrawn from the community and did not often leave the farm. These stress-related problems are a real concern for farm women.

One of the direct results of the decline in commodity prices is that the enterprise unit increases production of its commodities or diversifies into other commodities. This trend was evident in my study, and demonstrates the attempts made by the farming units to increase or maintain profits. The farms in the wheat-growing areas had diversified more than those in the grazing and mixed farming areas because wheat prices had been extremely marginal in the last few years. Of the 32 farms surveyed in the cropping area, only two had not changed or diversified their commodities. On the mixed enterprise farms, 12 had not changed their commodity base and 14 had. The predominant form of diversification reported by the women in the cropping area involved the production of crops as alternatives to wheat. These included canola, lupins, peas, oats, barley, lentils and clover. In the mixed farming region, seven women reported changes in cropping and seven reported stock diversification. The push is on to increase efficiency and production in order to increase or maintain the profit margin. Sometimes, however, despite increased production, profits remain marginal. Michelle noted: 'This last harvest, we had three times the amount of grain than what we had got the year before and we got $300 less than what we got paid the year before.'

Another strategy employed by farming units to maintain a profit margin is to expand the size of their holding. Twenty-four per cent of women questioned reported that they had purchased more land in the previous ten years. While the expansion of land holdings leads to increased levels of indebtedness, it also allows families to increase their production.

The constant pressure of low or negative profit margins, and the need to diversify and increase production, tie farms into a 'technological imperative', or the need to keep abreast of the latest developments in agriculture, in order that production is streamlined and a competitive edge is maintained.[3]

Another effect of the economic changes is a reduction in the amount of hired labour, a strategy which has been constantly referred to because of its impact on the role of women on farms. While not all of the farms surveyed employed labour, 40 per cent of women reported that reductions in the number of employed staff had been made or would be made. For many, this meant casual labour such as tractor drivers and shearers would not be employed and this labour would have to come from within the family. As Janet reported: 'We never did hire very many ... but now we just don't. It is just no, if we can't do it ourselves we don't do it.'

This reduction in hired labour, coupled with a striving for increased production, result in family members working longer hours. As well, women are being drawn into the farm labour process to substitute for the previously employed farm labour. As we saw in Chapter 7, several women mentioned their input into machinery driving, stockwork and rouseabouting during shearing time as a direct result of their replacing hired labour.

Reliance on a world market for sale of their products puts farming families in a precarious position when attempting to make production decisions. Because of the long production time dictated by nature, decisions need to be made some months in advance of selling a product. World market fluctuations mean that prices may change markedly during this time. This constraint was referred to by Anna, a young farm woman in the wheat-growing area. The family had diversified into other crops in order to survive the downturn in world wheat prices. She noted: 'They [husband and father-in-law] came home last night and said that the canola's gone down $40 a tonne, so it is going to be another bad year ... It is really frustrating and beyond your control. Like you try and do the right thing in mixing things and ...' Farming families are powerless to dictate terms for their products and are subject to external forces beyond their control.

One of the most prominent findings from this research is the importance of the family allowance (FA) and family allowance supplement (FAS) to the budgets of farm women with children. Particularly in the cropping areas, the FAS might be the only form of reliable income. As Debbie explained: 'Well, at the moment that is what we are living on for food ... that's our grocery money.' While not all women with children report that the family allowance and family allowance supplement are essential to their budget, most women do. The restriction on access by farming families to this and other forms of social security has been addressed elsewhere.[4] These restrictions have led to hardship being experienced by farming aged, such as Mona and her husband (discussed in Chapter 6), who are ineligible for aged pensions. For some young people from farming families, it has led to restrictions on access to education because they are ineligible for Austudy. Further restrictions on the family allowance will severely affect the ability of farming families to survive.

SUMMARY

The effects of economic restraint on farming families directly impinge on women and on the way they live their lives on farms. It is evident that changes have occurred between generations of farm women. Many of the labour tasks of older women had revolved around childcare, housework, farm enterprises and subsistence production. The changes on farms have led to the need for a source of cash income and this has usually meant that family members must look off the farm for paid work. In many cases, it has meant that the woman takes employment off the farm. Coupled with this move away from a concentration on subsistence tasks towards a need to seek off-farm work has been the developing recession in agriculture. This has added impetus to the need for off-farm work and for women to work in a number of different spheres. These include maintaining responsibility for household tasks, taking off-farm work where possible and often working on the farm as well as replacing hired labour.

Other effects of economic restraint include the need for women to be aware of financial management practices. Between generations, the need for business-management skills has increased, and it is more often the women who are taking charge of this area. Frances, an older farm woman, explained:

> It is a lot harder on their wives now because they are involved in the financial side of it and they know exactly what interest rates they are paying and all that sort of thing. And apart from rearing their children and doing all those things that you are called on to do now, apart from that, they have still got that anxiety which is really bad — that we never had at all ... But things are different now ... It's a lot harder on them I think.

Janet's story is an example of the reduced circumstances of many farm families and indicates the efforts being made by women to ensure farm viability.

Chapter 9
Janet's Story

Janet is 46 years old, married for 19 years and has three children. She and her husband are in partnership with her father-in-law and her three brothers-in-law, running the four farms on which the families live. Janet is halfway through her arts degree and her background is in nursing. Her husband left school after year 10 to work on the farm. They live in a grain-growing area of New South Wales. In recent years, their income has fallen dramatically as a result of the serious downturn in wheat prices. They have diversified their cropping program in an attempt to combat falling prices, and now grow canola, oats, field peas and barley as well as wheat. They also run sheep.

Janet is responsible for all the household tasks, 'except what I get the children to do', and she has always been the primary carer for her three teenage children. Janet keeps a vegetable garden and a small orchard, and preserves some of her produce and dries some of the fruit. She keeps poultry and is often required to rear lambs. Janet has provided meals for shearers and casual tractor drivers in the past. She remembers, 'I came home from my honeymoon to feed shearers. I sort of walked in the door, nearly, and had to prepare a meal for shearers.' She makes a lot of clothes for her children and, usually, the soft furnishings in her home. Janet is heavily involved in community work with her church and with the children's schools.

In order to diversify their income, the family bought into a local business. The downturn in the rural area has made it difficult for the business to succeed. Janet spends four or five days a week at the store, although she gets no pay for her work. Her husband also works off the farm doing occasional building and welding jobs on other farms in the district. Janet is also actively looking for nursing work and has put her name down at four different hospitals within a radius of 100 kilometres. She is now considering trying to find work in the city 120 kilometres away. Should she succeed, she will need to find accommodation in the city and spend time away from the family. 'Unfortunately, the financial situation is so bad that it has come to that ... we are living on our savings. The income from the farm has been ... a negative income.'

On the farm, Janet has always been involved with the machinery, although 'I do drive for the more simple tasks like ploughing. I never do for the harvest or the sowing.' Janet is often required to travel long distances for spare parts or other errands. She also helps with stockwork, but is rarely involved with decision-making and her husband does the farm books. To save on costs, Janet has replaced the shed hand at shearing time for the last few years. Because of her lack of a farming background, Janet sees her role on farm as a supportive one for her husband.

Janet's family's farm income has gone 'drastically down' in recent years. Coupled with rising farm input costs, the family is now in a precarious position. They no longer hire any labour. As well as diversifying their cropping program and expanding their land holding, the family has also steadily increased the amount of chemicals used in production, a development that disturbs Janet.

She and her husband have told their only son that he must seek a career away from the farm because they may not have a viable farm to pass on. Yet, because of their negative income, they do not know how they will be able to afford to educate their children without Austudy. Because of the farm assets, their children are assessed as ineligible for the benefit.

The downturn in agriculture has seriously affected many farm families like Janet's. She feels very sad about the current situation but is also philosophical.

It doesn't hurt any of us to have to say well, we just can't have new clothes. We just have to wear the old ones over and over and over ... That will probably do us a lot of good and help us to value our families more and value those sort of things more. But it does worry me that us and anybody else might get to the point of losing their means of earning a living.

CHAPTER 10

WHAT
DO I
CALL MYSELF?

> Every day you're answering phones, answering two-ways or people are ringing up, or you're going for this and that — so I guess I'm a part-time teacher, part-time farmworker, home carer, a mixed bag!
> *28-year-old New South Wales farm woman.*

Women on farms have a great deal of difficulty describing their role and identifying exactly what their occupation is. This chapter examines how they perceive themselves and their own work, whether they give value to their own farm input and whether they subscribe to a traditional sex-role stereotyped division of labour. In gauging the self-perceptions of the women interviewed, I asked several questions including whether their input made them feel important on the farm; whether they felt their husbands saw this as important; whether they felt their input was important to keeping the farm; what occupation they wrote down for themselves when filling out a form; whether they ever described themselves as farmers; what they saw as their own role on the farm and whether they felt women should be responsible for housework and men for farmwork. Each of these areas will be addressed separately.

WOMEN'S IMPORTANCE
ON THE FARM

All the women interviewed were asked whether 'your level of work made you feel important in the running of the farm'. The question was phrased this way to allow them to give value to every aspect of their work. Most women, however, saw the question as pertaining to farmwork and answered accordingly. Such an assumption suggests that most women do not see their household and childcare tasks as valuable input to the running of the farm. Of the 64 women questioned, thirty-eight (59 per cent) felt their level of work was important in the running of the farm and 41 per cent felt it was not. Significantly, only 14 of the 25 women under forty (56 per cent) felt that their level of work was important. Of those who didn't, three felt that although they know their own importance, other family members do not. This suggests that their own reassessment of their roles is not being matched by other family members. Joanne, commenting on this question, stated: 'I think I am the only one that thinks that way. I don't think anyone else in the family thinks like that.' Rhonda also felt this way: 'I guess I am important but I am not valued.' This negation of women's input by their own family is very discouraging indeed.

The reasons given by the women who do not see themselves as important often differed with age. For the older women, an adherence to a traditional division of labour made them feel that their input into the farm was unimportant, and some had also experienced displacement by sons. Younger women who see themselves as unimportant often refer to their responsibilities for young children and/or a partnership arrangement which excludes them.

Where appropriate, the women were then asked whether they felt their husbands saw them as important in the running of the farm. Notably, only 26 of the 59 married women (44 per cent) were able to answer positively without any hesitation. Many women appear to have more difficulty with this question. 'I think he does' was a typical response.

While it is unfair to make an assessment of the views of the husbands without actually questioning them, these figures suggest that many women feel that their husbands undervalue them, and either that farm husbands may not be viewing the work of women in a meaningful way or that the women answering the question do not value their own contribution. If, in fact, husbands are only viewing the direct farm labour as important to the running of the farm, then they are perhaps failing to appreciate the economic contributions women are making to the farm enterprise with their off-farm work, farmwork and subsistence production. Eleven of the 33 women (33 per cent) who felt their husbands saw their work as unimportant to the running of the farm or who were unsure worked off farm, and were thus generating income which, in most cases, was paying for the family's consumption costs.

Women were asked to comment on how important they felt their input was to *keeping* the family farm. Here, women were far more positive about their importance, with 73 per cent seeing their input as vital. Many saw their value in terms of their off-farm income and their potential to increase this work, while others were aware that they were saving the farm the cost of hired labour. Several women responded as did Louise, already employed part-time off farm, who saw her input as vital : '... if it came to the idea that we were going to lose it [the farm], then I would go back to work full-time to help supplement it'. Others see themselves as saving the cost of labour. Karen, who also worked off the farm for 25 hours a week, reported: '... if I didn't help on the farm anyway, we would have to pay someone'.

Most saw their chief importance in the fact that they kept things running smoothly. Helen, like many others, felt she was vitally important in keeping her husband motivated and supported: '... he wouldn't be able to spend the time on it he does either because I look after everything else'.

WOMEN'S JOB DESCRIPTIONS

W omen were asked what would be an accurate description of themselves and their duties if they had to write down their occupation. The answers to this question illustrate the great difficulties farm women have in labelling themselves, and may explain why they are so underrepresented in official statistics. Because they are involved in so many areas, this question of labelling causes huge problems for women. In fact, many women resolve it by looking at what they spend most of their time on, which is home duties, and labelling themselves accordingly. Twenty-eight of the 59 married women (47 per cent) described themselves as having 'home duties' and/or 'being a mother'. Surprisingly, this included 14 women who worked off the farm. Joanne, for instance, reported that she describes herself as a housewife even though she works off the farm, because: 'It's a subconscious thing, I'm sure, because it's so much, my job is so much of what I do in the community anyway ... it just gets lumped in with everything else.' Like many employed women, her caring and nurturing role extends into her employment, and she views her job as much of the same. In fact, only 35 per cent of the working women label themselves in terms of their off-farm occupation. Megan, a casual teacher, called herself: 'Domestic engineer? My duties are just general duties of being a mother and homemaker and taxi driver and all those things.'

Five women referred, half-jokingly, to themselves as 'dog's body' or 'slave.' Only 35 per cent of the women questioned outlined their occupation in terms of farmwork, and for most of these, it was a combination of 'home duties' and 'farm duties'. The women were questioned further about this and asked if 'you ever describe yourselves as a farmer'. In fact, 21 women (35 per cent) said they did. For some of them, this was only when they had to fill out forms or for taxation purposes. For example, Hannah replied honestly: 'No, but my tax accountant does.'

The remaining 65 per cent never describe themselves as farmers. The difficulty women have describing themselves as farmers seems to stem from the fact that they, for the most part, married into farming and have always viewed farming as their husband's occupation. Beth put it this way: '[My husband] has always been responsible for making the final decision. When he has been away for periods of time ... it has been completely different ... I have been totally responsible for going around and checking all the stuff. It is just a completely different feeling that if I owned the farm or if I was the one that was totally responsible then I would call myself a farmer. Society and everyone else sees me as a farmer's wife'. Thirty-four per cent of the women interviewed feel this is the case. Six other women, such as Jean, felt it was because they were not doing the hard, physical work. 'Because I am not out there digging the ground and doing the work.'

Six women felt they could not describe themselves as farmers because of the partnership arrangements. Five felt they had their own occupation. Others, such as Sue, saw themselves as helpers or farmer's wives and could not identify themselves as farmers: 'I have never really thought of myself as a farmer. I am just there to help. I suppose that I do a bit of everything. I am a gardener, a housewife — so there is a lot of things you could call yourself.'

That this view of themselves is reinforced by society and their spouses is illustrated by the women's responses. Kristen, who had changed her self-perception in 1986, possibly because of the farm women's rally in which she was heavily involved, commented:

> I always describe myself as a farmer. This goes back to 1986 when [I had to] put occupation [on a tax form]. Before that I used to put housewife and I don't know why I did that. I don't know why I changed. But now I put farmer and grazier. And I was filling out a form putting farmer and grazier last year on a form and [my husband] said to me half-joking, half-serious, "You are not a farmer and grazier, you are a housewife", and I said, "I am a farmer and grazier" and he said, "I am going to cross that out and put that you are a housewife". And I said, "Well, you cross that out and I will do nothing, absolutely nothing but work in the house." He didn't cross it out and he has never complained again.

Very few of the women have learnt to value their contribution as much as Kristen has, but as she says: 'You really have to stand up for yourself and you have to put a value on yourself at some stage of your life. I think you always do, but you have to actually articulate that to other people and to your husband.'

Significantly, all of the widows interviewed described themselves as farmers, but had only begun to do this after their husbands had died and they themselves took control of the running of the farm. Several other women felt they had been able to describe themselves as farmers, at least on official forms, only after legal arrangements had been made that included them. These perceptions of themselves as farmers had less to do with actual work undertaken by the women than it did with legal arrangements and society's perceptions of women's roles. Women are discounted because of the way they enter farming and because of their subsequent secondary status in the enterprise. Rural ideology does not recognise their efforts and contributions because 'farmwork' is often defined in terms of hard, physical labour which prevents women's contributions in so many areas being recognised and valued.

The women were asked to comment on how they viewed their own role on the farm. An interesting assortment of terms was used by the women to describe their role. These included 'helper' (ten responses), 'support' (eight responses), 'Jack of all trades' (four responses), 'sounding board' (three responses), 'backstop,' 'coordinator' and 'back-up' (two responses each), as well as 'offsider,' 'dog's body,' 'everybody's slave,' 'rouseabout,' 'mum', and 'provider'. That women feel subordinate on the farm is evident from their answers to this question. If they are to seek a more central and equitable place for themselves, they must change the way they see their role on the farm.

THE SEXUAL DIVISION
OF LABOUR

W omen were asked to comment on whether they felt women should be responsible for the house and men for the farm in order to assess whether they supported a traditional division of roles. In fact, 56 per cent of women agreed with a traditional assignment of roles, while 44 per cent felt that the assignment of tasks should be more flexible. The women in the more isolated cropping areas were more likely to agree to traditional roles.

When these responses were categorised according to age, they showed that women under 40 tended to support a more flexible role allocation, and women aged 40 or over usually supported a more traditional role allocation. Seventy-two per cent of younger women as opposed to 26 per cent of older women favoured flexibility in work roles. This dramatic change in role expectations from one generation to the next is a result of increased educational levels for women, the increase in the number of areas in which women are now working and changes in community expectations concerning women's roles. Many of the younger women agree with Megan. 'I don't believe there are women's jobs and men's jobs. I think whoever sort of fits to do it — or whatever is suitable for a particular family. I think that men or women are capable of doing either jobs.'

Older women were more likely to agree with Joan, who felt that: '... there are some defined roles, definitely, and I think that women are better at raising children and doing housework than men ... I think [farmwork] is men's work, I don't really think it is women's work ... there are certain things that men are better at and other things that women are better at.'

Such a major change in role expectations by younger women has not been matched by similar changes on the part of their husbands. Farm husbands, who still largely support a traditional assignment of roles, appear to see their wives as domestically centred and do not help with household tasks in any significant way. Such differing expectations are the cause of a great deal of frustration for farm women and, in some instances, reduce their satisfaction with their relationship. Where older women found comfort from fitting in with traditional and dependent roles with their husbands, the majority of younger women found little satisfaction in a traditional assignment of roles and often expressed antagonism about such arrangements.

THE VIEW OF WOMEN
OUTSIDE THE FARM GATE

W hen asked to comment on the place of women in agriculture generally, 75 per cent noted that women's place on the farm is very important. Their need to replace hired labour and/or work off the farm, and to look after the farm books were factors mentioned in support of their increasing importance. Ruth, for example, stated: 'I see my place as changing. I think being home to facilitate cups of tea and preserving the fruit and that sort of thing has gone out the door.' Robin felt that women have always had a huge input into family farming over the years which has gone unrecognised, but that now their contribution is vital.

> I can see it in tough times, particularly. It's so important, because so many women, not just the fact that they are at home and cooking lunches and doing things like that, but their actual physical input. The fact that so many of them do the bookwork and make so many financial decisions … I think a lot of them have a lot better financial understanding of the business than the husbands …

The constraints, both ideological and structural, were mentioned by many women when discussing the place of women in agriculture. Carol felt that: '… more women have to get into high places. I honestly believe that women have not done enough. Their potential hasn't been fully realised because men are blocking them.' Kristen, eloquent as ever, summed up her feelings about women in agriculture, and the feelings of many others, thus: 'They are a tremendous unseen, unrecognisable force. They contribute a tremendous amount to the wealth, the stability and economic success of the farm. Added to that, they contribute a tremendous amount to the community, to their schools and their organisational skills — and I think mostly it is unrecognised.'

To explore their ideas about women's place in agriculture, women were asked to comment on how they feel women are portrayed in the agricultural literature, particularly the *Land* newspaper, the largest farm newspaper in New South Wales. Forty-seven per cent of women felt that the portrayal of women is okay and 53 per cent felt that women are misrepresented or presented in roles that are too traditional. Those who had no concerns included Vicky. 'I think the *Land* does a pretty good job actually. You can't take away the fact that women have different interests to men, and when the *Land* does a whole series on the CWA Cookery Contest, well, the women read the *Land*, so I guess they're entitled to that sort of coverage.' Those who had concerns about the coverage of women included Sue. 'It perpetuates the traditional role as far as they are mostly in cooking columns. The CWA doesn't seem to do much to my way of thinking about promotion of women in any other role … Sometimes, the media I find offensive, I guess, in the way they portray women in the country.'

While women over 40 were more likely to have no problems with women's portrayal in the agricultural literature (41 per cent were concerned and 59 per cent were not), 68 per cent of the women under 40 had concerns, while only 32 per cent did not. This appears to suggest a changing consciousness developing among younger farm women, although this is far more developed in the less isolated areas.

To gauge further the perceptions of the women in the study concerning the place of women in agriculture, they were asked to comment on whether they felt there were any barriers to women owning and controlling land. Again, women were divided on this issue, and age and area were factors in the division. Older women tended to perceive no difficulties for women seeking ownership and control of land (77 per cent for 40 or over; 44 per cent for under 40), and this despite the fact that very few women own and run farms unless they are widows.

Those who felt there were no barriers did not discuss structural factors but often named widows they know who were running farms successfully. Those who felt there were barriers spoke of patrilineal inheritance, isolation, problems with lending institutions and the level of ostracism women might face if they took on such a role. Toni mentioned the institutional barriers women face. 'I think there are a lot of financial ones and a lot of probably legal ones and there is also a lot of in-built ones within our society. I have a friend whose husband died last year and the problems that she encountered within the legal system and within the farm management systems were monumental. Monumental!' Again, the replies to this question demonstrate the differences in attitude between generations of farm women, and are evidence of an emerging consciousness among younger women about wider structural and societal barriers to women's incorporation into agriculture.

Women were also asked whether there are barriers to women's employment in rural areas, both in towns and on farms. Sixty-nine per cent of women felt there were barriers, but again, there is an age differential, with 88 per cent of women under 40 agreeing that there were barriers and only 56 per cent for women 40 and over. Differences in how younger and older women interpreted the question affected their responses. The older women often interpreted this question in terms of social attitudes now, compared to when they themselves were young. Consequently, they were accurate in their assessment that the resistance to women being employed in towns had diminished, and so there were fewer barriers to women's employment off the farm. Younger women more often viewed this question as pertaining to job opportunities, which, for them, are few and far between, and so they perceived enormous barriers to women's employment off the farm. As well, they often mentioned the social barriers which act to prevent women being employed on farms, the most obvious area of employment in rural areas.

These more general questions produced significant data on the interviewees' perceptions of the place of women in agriculture and rural society generally. Overwhelmingly, women were aware of the increasingly important role of women in maintaining the viability of the farm. However, the accuracy of their portrayal in the agricultural media is more likely to be questioned by the younger women. The traditional stereotyping mentioned by many of these women was felt to inaccurately reflect their own lives. Younger women were also more likely to question the structural barriers to women's entry into farming and the lack of opportunity for them to be employed on farms and in towns. As Sharon put it: 'The blokes don't like employing women to go and drive tractors and drive trucks and load hay. It is okay for their wives to do it, but you don't pay somebody else's wife to do it.' The data presented here provide evidence of an emerging consciousness among the younger farm women who were aware of, and beginning to question, the structural barriers which confront them.

EXPECTATIONS FOR
THEIR CHILDREN

W hen questioned about the expectations for their children, their commitment to the enterprise and the possibility of passing on the farm to their children, some quite significant findings emerged. In fact, it appears that women remain very traditional in their thinking and do not question the patrilineal system of transferring the farm. As Sarah Whatmore has demonstrated in her British study, women still act to 'channel' property rights to the next male heir and do not use their own legal status in an enterprise in any independent way.[1] What did emerge from this study, however, is that women are less committed to preserving the enterprise and passing it on to the next generation. As intergenerational transfer is so heavily dependent on women's facilitation of the process, this represents a significant finding and may signal changes in future ownership. Another important aspect to emerge is the commitment of the women to ensuring that their sons are educated off the farm in another skill or trade before they are allowed to return.

Women of all ages saw future inheritors of their land as sons or grandsons. Only seven women mentioned daughters as possible inheritors, and this was usually in the context of an equal inheritance share with sons, rather than being left the farm as an occupational choice. Two women who had only daughters saw no future transfer of land taking place; rather, they would sell the farm. Women gave various reasons for excluding daughters from inheritance of land, including the fact that their daughter(s) would marry and leave, that they would be educated for something else, that the work was too hard and that they did not want to set their daughters up for social ostracism. Such reasons were given even when daughters were older than sons and exhibited a great deal of interest and enthusiasm for farmwork. This is an illustration of the power of male dominance in agriculture. Often, however, the reasons women supported the ideology were because they were more ambitious for daughters and saw them escaping the hard work of farming. For example, Michelle reported: 'I see [my son] as a farmer, yes. [My daughter], I really hope she goes further. I would like her to become a lawyer or something like that ...' However, the strength of cultural mores led most women to feel intuitively that they had to protect their daughters from social isolation. Ruth put it this way:

> I personally don't like the idea of [my daughter] being a farmer and nor does [my husband]. But his are sexist reasons. I suppose to a degree mine are too, in that looking at the females around that have been farmers, that almost seem misfits ... Farmers like to deal with men. Men like to deal with farmers. I think it would be a hard row to hoe ...

The strong commitment on the part of the women to ensuring that sons who do want to be farmers be trained in something else first represents a departure from previously accepted practice. The hard times experienced by farming families now have produced a strong determination in these women to ensure their sons have other options. This will mean that sons — in the isolated areas, at least — will inevitably have to leave home for a time in order to attend university, agricultural college or TAFE. Whether they return remains to be seen. Several women reported they were actively encouraging their sons to give up any idea of farming. The hardship and financial strain of farming in Australia are something they do not want to see their children doing. As Pam explained:

'We have told them [our two sons] that they are going to have to go out and get jobs — there is just no future here.' Many women expressed similar sentiments, and 22 per cent of women reported that their farms will be sold.

When asked whether they were committed to farming, 28 per cent of women said they were not at all committed. That eight of these women are under 40 (32 per cent of the women under 40 in the study) suggests that some women are losing their enthusiasm for their role as facilitator of patrilineal inheritance practices, and are less than enthusiastic about the hard work they are involved in to ensure farm viability. Should financial hardship continue, there may be dramatic changes ahead in the social relations of agricultural production.

The commitment of women to educating their children was demonstrated in this study. All women expect their children (or grandchildren) to seek a higher level of education than themselves (or their children). However, there was an area difference in expectations of women as to the level they would like their children to achieve. Eighty per cent of women in the more populated areas would like their children to have tertiary education; and 20 per cent, at least HSC level. In the isolated cropping areas, 48 per cent would like their children to reach HSC level; and 52 per cent, tertiary. The lower expectations of some isolated women are, no doubt, a result of limited access to tertiary institutions and the isolating effect of distance.

WOMEN'S EMERGING CONSCIOUSNESS

The results presented in this chapter suggest that younger women are not as accepting of prescribed patriarchal gender roles as the older women interviewed, and that it appears they are developing a consciousness of gender issues. Therefore, the analysis of the data surrounding questions concerning attitudes to feminism and political orientation became highly significant. Were younger farm women becoming less conservative, and if so, were they becoming more attuned to a feminist philosophy? In fact, it was clear from their responses to the question 'Would you say you were conservative, radical or somewhere in between?' that younger women are moving away from a conservative point of view. Although none saw themselves as radical, 80 per cent (compared with 44 per cent of older women) were emphatic that they were not conservative. Many of the younger women felt constrained by the ideology of the community in which they lived from openly declaring themselves to have more radical points of view. As Barbara put it: 'I'm probably basically conservative but … I was probably more radical before. Being in a small town has made me more conservative because I … suppose I've become more self-conscious.' Several younger women agreed with Barbara and also with Toni who said: 'Whilst my own personal views could almost be termed radical, I am not prepared to sort of make an issue — make a statement outside my own family much about them.'

The constraints these women feel, and the threat of some measure of social ostracism that may follow an open declaration of their views, cause them to remain politically inactive. The pressures of an ideology which assigns them to wifehood and prescribes a narrow role for them make it very difficult for farm women to assert themselves as individuals. In fact, only five of the 64 women interviewed feel they can claim to be politically active. This marginality that women experience in rural areas makes their responses to the question on their attitudes to feminism highly significant. Was feminism attractive to them and did it offer them a way of analysing the patriarchal gender roles that confront them? Perhaps not surprisingly, many of these farm women were very wary of feminism and saw it as alien to their lives because of its urban bias and failure to take up issues which concern rural women.

Fifty-six per cent of younger women had a favourable opinion of feminism and 44 per cent were unimpressed; while 36 per cent of older women had a positive opinion of feminism and 64 per cent were against it. Older women, such as Mona, are more likely to reject feminism outright. 'I don't believe in them. Greenies and all this. I think they are idiots.'

Many mentioned they have always felt equal and so they see the women's movement only causing disruption. These women have always maintained a level of private power based on the integral nature of their role on farm, and see feminism threatening this power. Nevertheless, younger women and some older women are aware of the benefits that the women's movement has brought to their lives. As Kate notes: 'It gave me confidence in myself and my own ability. I am sure that will have affected other country women.'

However, many women openly reject feminism because of the way it has been presented in the media, because it is perceived as having little relevance in their lives and because of the threat of ostracism for anyone who is seen as a strong feminist. Others have little time for feminism because they have always felt equal or because they feel that men and women are 'different' and so cannot be equal. Some women who are better informed about feminism and what the women's movement has achieved for them feel there is a need for feminist ideologies to permeate rural culture. Vicky feels feminism would benefit farm women because: 'There are a lot of farm women who are still treated as "the drudge" around the place. She is there to bear the children, to provide the meals, to provide a hell of a lot of work on the farm but she is given no place in the decision-making process whatever ...'

However, a general lack of understanding of feminism pervaded the women's responses in the study, and suggests, firstly, that feminist issues are not being adequately presented or are being openly disparaged by the media, and secondly, that feminists have been guilty of an urban focus that has excluded rural women.

SUMMARY

That patriarchal gender relations and male dominance in agriculture still structure women's lives on farms, despite the enormous changes that have taken place in agriculture, is evident from the data presented here. Gender prescriptions have merely been rewritten to incorporate new conditions, but not without a muttering of discontent among younger women, at least. The data presented in this chapter have illustrated a generational change in attitudes among farm women and an obvious move away from both traditional conservatism and adherence to traditional role stereotyping, at least in theory. While older women still support a division of labour based on sex, having gained a great deal of satisfaction from the different but dependent roles they shared with their husbands, younger women express frustration and antagonism at being expected to continue to support, in theory, the idea of traditional stereotyping. In practice, they are working on farm replacing hired labour, off the farm to maintain farm viability, in the community to ensure its continued survival and at home, taking most of the responsibility for domestic work.

Farm women are struggling with problems of identity, and their own perceptions of themselves are not always matched by those around them. Women are aware of their valuable input towards keeping the family farm viable but are often uncertain about their husband's perception of their worth. They invest a great deal of time and energy in many areas both on and off the farm, and yet, many still describe themselves as having 'home duties'. Despite their input, which they themselves see as vital, they describe their role on the farm in subordinate terms. Only 28 per cent of the women interviewed have ever felt comfortable describing themselves as farmers, despite their level of work or their legal status, and yet, most of the younger women are now denying any validity to traditional sex roles. The self-perceptions of farm women about their own roles appear not to be influenced by their level of off-farm work, the number of young children they have or their farm background and education. Those variables which do appear to affect women's self-perception include their legal status in the enterprise, the structure of the partnership arrangement and the presence or absence of a male partner. Women involved in extended family partnerships are more likely to feel excluded, and women who are widowed assume a perception of themselves as 'farmers'. However, expectations appear to be changing, and younger women are questioning their ideological assignment to the domestic sphere despite the fact that there have not been corresponding changes in the way the role of women is viewed within their own family or within the farming communities in which they live.

The emerging consciousness of younger women is evident in their awareness of their own private power; their move away from conservatism; their awareness of, and antagonism towards, the traditional portrayal of women in the agricultural literature; their understanding of the structural barriers to women owning and controlling land; and their lessening commitment to facilitating patrilineal transfer of land. Yet, these women are still struggling with problems of identity as a result of the ideological climate surrounding the business of farming. While younger farm women are moving away from traditional conservatism, many remain unconvinced that feminism can offer them a way of understanding their own marginality. Their struggle has not been helped by a biased media presentation and a lack of focus on the unique problems of rural women.

CHAPTER 11

MAKING FARM WOMEN VISIBLE

I think women's place could be very, very large and very, very important
if men let it be ... I think we need to educate them to an understanding
that we actually have brains and could be their biggest asset.
39 year-old New South Wales farm woman.

I n detailing the lives of farm women, it has been important to allow them to speak for themselves about their experiences and their contributions to agriculture, to their communities and to their families. The structural arrangements that surround the business of farming have acted to confine women to a secondary role, to obscure the significance of their contributions and to silence their concerns. This book has examined the way farming families, and the communities in which they live, legitimate women's domestic role and negate the value of their other contributions.

The extent of women's economic contributions has not been officially recognised to date because of the narrow, business-oriented definition of 'farmwork'; the operation of patriarchal gender relations; the power differential between farm partners and because of ideologies which act to diminish women's efforts. Several women interviewed report feeling undervalued or taken for granted inside the family as well as beyond the farm gate. This undervaluing operates at the highest level with official statistics failing to recognise and report accurate figures representing women's input into agriculture. The undervaluing continues with significant business and professional people with whom women do business, who make it plain that they see women in agriculture as irrelevant despite their legal status, and more intimately and devastatingly, it often continues within their own family. As Ruth Gasson suggests, '...habitual minimising of the wife's contribution to farming is a logical outcome of the low value which society places on women's domestic work'.[1] That this undervaluing is internalised by many women is substantiated by the number of women who refer to their efforts in subordinate terms such as 'help', 'support' and so on.

What we must acknowledge from the evidence presented here is that the operation of family farming is dependent on the flexibility and multiple activities of all family members, including women, and that the persistence of this type of production depends on just such flexibility.[2] Without the non-waged contributions of women and indeed, their off-farm income-generating activity, family farming could not continue in this country. As Gasson states, '...family farming cannot continue without the compliance of women'[3]. However, if a realistic value were to be placed on their work, it would underlie the fact that family farming is far less efficient and competitive than we have been led to believe. As Sally Shortall notes in her Irish study, 'If the farm wife's contribution were to be acknowledged and fair retribution made, it would place huge strains on the farming industry.'[4] That women have always made a significant economic contribution to family farming in this country is amply demonstrated in this work. While their contribution has changed from subsistence and on-farm cottage-type industries to an on-farm, off-farm combination of activities, what has not changed is the lack of recognition, the undervaluing and the discounting of these efforts.

The evidence presented here suggests that the continued compliance of younger farm women may be dependent on a number of factors, chief among these being recognition of their status and contribution, both legally and formally. As well, a realignment of gender expectations will be necessary if women are to continue generating income and replacing hired labour.

One of the factors in women's subordination has been the lack of women-focused theories of society before the development of feminist theorising in the 1960s and 1970s. My research, informed by a feminist perspective, has allowed farm women to speak for themselves and to emerge from the shadows of official neglect. What is evident from this research is that farm women are constrained by patriarchal gender relations, and by rural ideology.

GENDER, POWER
AND IDEOLOGY

W hen studying the lives of farm women, one cannot ignore the effects of gender stereotyping and the patriarchal relations which rule women's lives. As Gretchen Poiner suggests, gender divisions are the most intransigent of all social divisions, and their strength in this country has acted to ensure men's cultural dominance and women's subordination.[5] However, perhaps in no other industry do such stringent gender-role definitions operate. Women marrying into a farming family (and this is the predominant mode of entry into farming for women) marry not only their husband, but often they also marry into a family system which is hierarchically structured across generations, so that they are often placed in a position subordinate to their husband's parents and brothers. Farm women marry into a traditionally defined role where they are expected to take full responsibility for the household and childcare and be available to help on farm, run errands, do the books and any other job that arises. The expectation that they will be available extends to women who take part-time off-farm work. Small concessions are made, but usually the work schedule is rearranged to fit around the woman's off-farm work hours. The expectation that women are available to 'help' and will give priority to farm tasks has not been seriously challenged in rural families and communities. The discrepancies between the actions of the women interviewed and their stated preferences suggest farm women's choices are blocked. That all women take responsibility for housework and childcare, regardless of any other variable, suggests that these occupations have been imposed as part of their subordinate gender role. All women assume these responsibilities, despite the fact that many report they would rather be doing more farmwork or off-farm work. Many report being restricted from pursuing their choices by a lack of time because of their domestic responsibilities. That they were not relieved of the responsibilities even when they work on the farm or off the farm again indicates a lack of choice for women in the allocation of tasks on farm. As Shortall discovered in her study of Irish farm women, women will avoid objecting to the imposed conditions and obstruction of their choices because they wish to avoid conflict and friction within their family and within the wider community.[6]

The continuation of the traditional expectations for women is reinforced by the rural ideology of 'wifehood', which relegates women to a subordinate, 'helping' position, and by the socialisation of farm men, which leads them to expect that women will perform a traditional role. As well, the fact that farm men are, on the whole, less well educated than farm women may mean they are not exposed to alternative roles between the sexes. On the other hand, younger, university-educated women marrying into a farming family, who have experienced less clearly defined role divisions in the city, report that they find the traditional expectations imposed upon them particularly irksome.

The operation of gender stereotyping and expectations extends beyond the farm gate into the rural communities in which these women live. Despite their other workloads, women are expected to represent the family in a voluntary capacity in a number of areas but particularly within the schools. Without their voluntary efforts, many vital rural services would cease to exist. Yet, women report finding it difficult to find the time and resources to continue this work.

This research has highlighted the significance of inter- and intragenerational partnership arrangements as an important factor in women's marginalisation in farming systems. The women in more isolated cropping areas are far more likely to be involved in such arrangements than the women surveyed in more populous areas. The former group of women reports feeling particularly disadvantaged because their involvement on the farm is not always welcome, although they are still expected to be the 'go-fer' and 'help' when needed. They report being in a subordinate position to fathers-in-law and/or brothers-in-law, and because their financial situation is often precarious, it is often the woman's off-farm income that supports her immediate family in this situation. Furthermore, their involvement in farm decision-making is often non-existent. In some cases, the family's yearly income is decided in meetings from which the woman is excluded. Such arrangements produce a great deal of anger and frustration for younger women, and arguably, reduce their satisfaction with their marriage.

However, the powerlessness felt by women in this situation is often matched by a powerlessness on the part of their husbands. As Anna, who had been married 14 years, noted when asked whether she was involved in the partnership with her husband, brothers-in-law and father-in-law:

> It has just — last year — it was put in, yes ... It's taken a while, yes that's a very sore point! I thought when I've come from a family — you know, Mum and Dad — most things were in combined names. They have a fairly equal type of marriage. I was originally from the city ... then came out here. When I came out here, it was very male-dominated terrain, and I thought as soon as we got married we would work in a partnership ... So I've struggled to get my name put in the partnership ... [My husband] seemed to have no power. It was sort of up to his ... father ... I don't think [my husband] fought hard enough for it. He just went along with whatever father-in-law said. And I think it was mainly because of the tax reason that they finally ... the tax accountant suggested it, I think mainly for tax reasons.

Anna went on to explain that she is not involved in land ownership, although it is her off-farm income that is being used to do up their house on the farm. Many of the women whose husbands were tied up in family arrangements report similar stories and resultant frustration and anger. That young Australian farm women are not alone in their appraisal of the existing regime is evident from the literature. In England, Sarah Whatmore also found that the situation was difficult, '... particularly [for] younger women, for whom the gender regime of family farming is becoming increasingly archaic and insupportable in the light of developments on the wider social canvas of gender relations'.[7]

When one examines the situation of the widows in this study, it becomes evident that reactions or power differentials change under abnormal conditions. Consequently, widows are able to behave differently when the power structures are relaxed. All but one of the widows interviewed attended farm organisation meetings after their husbands died. As well, farm business was directed to them and farm production decisions became their responsibility when they were widowed. By contrast, few farm wives attend farm meetings and few are involved in decision-making. Their exclusion from these activities legitimises male dominance and involvement, and reinforces the existing order. Evidence can be gleaned which suggests that the more powerful group — in this case, male farmers — has not acted to alter the mobilisation of bias against women in agriculture. For example, despite the obvious absence of women from farm organisations, no action or research has been undertaken by these organisations to examine the causes of women's exclusion.

Patrilineal inheritance practices are indicative of the subordinate position of women; they effectively disinherit women and reinforce their subordinate status. That most women in this study support the idea of patrilineal inheritance demonstrates they concur with their own secondary position, and they are aware that any support for a contrary position would create conflicts for themselves or their daughters. A consequence of their concurrence, however, is a continuation of the secondary position of women in agriculture, a reduction of choice for women and a narrow definition of women's legitimate activities.

There has been much debate in the literature about the effects of women's off-farm work on the power differentials operating within the farm family.[8] Cornelia Flora and Sue Johnson suggest that women's income-producing potential must lead to their higher status within the family. More pessimistically, Gasson suggests that wives may be simply adding to their workload in order to subsidise the farm family without gaining any compensatory increase in power. The findings from this study tend to support Gasson's view that women are merely adding to their already heavy workload, and no shifts in power are evident. In fact, some women suggest they are working off the farm to give themselves an area where they have authority and influence in their own right free from the gender regime surrounding family farming. The power differentials are particularly difficult to challenge when women are involved in farms with inter- and intragenerational arrangements. Working off the farm does little to change such systems and merely removes women temporarily from a situation in which they feel marginalised.

Women in this study report that little help with domestic tasks is forthcoming from family members. This suggests that male family members view women as domestically orientated and subordinate within the family, and that gender bias is being perpetuated despite the objections and concerns of many women. This perception of women continues off the farm as well, with many agricultural organisations failing to recognise the knowledge and skills of women away from the domestic sphere. Despite the fact that farm women are more likely to have achieved higher education standards than their husbands, this has not translated into a sharing of domestic tasks in the private sphere, nor has it resulted in women being taken seriously in the public sphere. Traditional farm organisations are overlooking the input of women, despite the fact that it is women who often have intimate knowledge of the financial affairs and workings of the farm by doing the books and managing the business enterprise. In fact, many farm families may be ignoring their greatest asset, the daughter-in-law with tertiary qualifications who has spent time establishing her career before marriage.

Nonetheless, it should be pointed out that many women support the existing gender regime which renders them invisible in the public arena, and report finding great satisfaction in their assigned role because of their influence, or 'private power', within their family unit This influence is based, firstly, on their integral role in linking the private and productive sphere, and secondly, on their primacy in nurturing and caring for the family. While this power within their limited sphere should not be discounted, it should not be viewed as a compensatory power justifying women's exclusion from public areas of authority and influence.

Male dominance, 'wifehood' and women's subsumption within the family act to reinforce and legitimate the division of roles by gender, gender inequalities and the existing power structure. Consequently, the designation of men's work as superior, the relegation of women to the private sphere, the undervaluing of women's work and the acceptance of women's public invisibility are reinforced and legitimated by existing social structures and cultural mores.

This work has demonstrated that, generally, farm women are ambivalent about feminist ideologies, and that feminism is not always seen as an answer for women. Surprisingly, even the younger women showed a degree of ambivalence about feminism that had not been evident in their responses to questions on feminist issues, such as the division of labour in the home. During the course of this research, I was aware of the unfavourable media presentation of feminist issues in rural areas and of the acceptance of this view by many women. Feminism is generally disparaged in rural communities. Community education may advance the cause of women and highlight the gains made by women as a result of the second wave of feminism and feminist research in this country. Furthermore, government grant bodies, such as the Rural Access Program and the National Agenda for Women Program, should look towards funding research into rural and farm women's concerns. To date, they have largely been ignored by government funding bodies.

It is, however, evident that the urban focus of feminism has been a major reason why rural women discount its value and, indeed, are threatened by feminist pronouncements. The failure of urban feminists to understand the importance of 'family' within family farm production, and their assumption that an urban model of family is valid in rural society, have led to an undifferentiated attack which has alienated many rural women. The importance placed on family by women involved in family enterprises ensures that attacks made on the family by urban feminists will be seen as a threat by rural women.

FARM WOMEN'S LIVES

This book has illustrated the changing work roles for women on farms over the last 50 years. Women have moved from a very traditional sexual division of labour, where each partner relied on the interdependent efforts of the other in their own sphere, to a more flexible allocation of family labour outside the household, although not within. The traditional and prescribed role allocation, remembered with some satisfaction by many of the older women, allowed them dominance in their own sphere and gave them a sense of place. As well as their private, domestic work, many were directly involved in production with their own on-farm industries, such as poultry, egg and cream production and butter-making. This study has uncovered evidence that Australian farm women contributed significantly to meeting consumption costs within the farm household for much of the last 50 years. That this evidence has come from the two different and geographically distant areas investigated suggests a widespread trend in which women took responsibility for generating income and covering consumption costs within their enterprises. This research corroborates Deborah Fink's United States study, and suggests that this phenomenon has wider relevance not yet incorporated into studies of agricultural production in Western countries.[9] The business-oriented, commodity-production-driven approach to agricultural history and statistics has ignored the multidimensional aspects of farm family livelihood.

The fact that women enter farming, for the most part, through marriage has ensured male dominance in agriculture. Women's secondary place in the family and the enterprise, and the role of cross-generational partnerships in reducing the significance of women's contributions, are factors not readily acknowledged in agriculture. Yet, the structure of the farm family arrangement dictates the way women will live and work within the family and on the farm. Their limited power both on the farm and in the community is a direct result of their inferior position in the farm family.

Chapters 6, 7 and 8 have shown that women are active participants in many areas of 'work'. By moving away from a business-oriented definition of 'work' and by including the tasks in which women are involved in a comprehensive definition of farmwork, it is possible to expose the full extent of their labour, and to argue that much of this work makes an economic contribution to the enterprise. A thorough examination of the domestic economy of farms is necessary in order to appreciate the value of women's contributions to the farm economy as a whole.

Their involvement in subsistence production, on-farm work, off-farm work and voluntary community work gives value to their families, to their enterprises and to their communities. Until there is a fundamental shift in assigning value to all forms of work, women's efforts will remain invisible, because much of what they do is not directly related to production.

The changes in agricultural production technologies and the difficult economic circumstances in which farm families are operating have seen major shifts in women's work roles on farms. While there is much support in this study for the notion that agriculture has become 'defeminised' as women relinquish their productive agricultural industries and as technological advances encroach on agricultural production, there are, however, unique aspects in the Australian condition which must be noted. Like their overseas counterparts, Australian women have been moved out of their own industries and have moved from a central place in agricultural production to the periphery, where they perform tasks such as 'go-fering', which act to facilitate the productive tasks of men. Yet, studies in other countries, where subsidisation of agriculture is the norm, suggest that women have moved out of production. However, this move has been facilitated by increasing numbers of hired labour.[10] In contrast, the majority of women in this Australian study report that hired labour on their farms is being reduced because of the cost–price squeeze and reduction in commodity prices. Consequently, many women report being drawn into such tasks as machinery driving and rouseabouting in shearing sheds, replacing previously hired labour. Their incorporation into these tasks is, however, still in a subordinate role, and many previously male tasks have been split along gender lines so that men often perform the more critical tasks and women the less critical. The adoption of bigger and more sophisticated machinery has made it more difficult for women to be integrally involved in these tasks because of their lack of knowledge and affinity with these machines. Nevertheless, women are more likely to perform livestock tasks, and their increasing involvement in livestock management is a direct result of a reduction in hired labour. While women are taking on more of this work and many are also generating income off the farm, a realignment of domestic responsibilities has not taken place. Individual farming families and the agricultural community as a whole may have to re-examine the increasingly difficult and diverse expectations being placed on women in their secondary role as 'helper'.

The younger women in this study have made it clear that their acceptance of traditional stereotyping is at best reluctant. This research demonstrates that younger women have moved away from a conservative viewpoint and from an acceptance of prescribed roles which previously defined the identity of farm women. Many women express forthright views on their own importance and the importance of women in agriculture generally. However, their exclusion from public political forums in agriculture, for the various reasons set out in Chapter 5, has meant that women do not have a platform for making their positions and opinions visible. The rural women's network developing in this country holds the best hope of providing such a forum for Australian farm women, and may allow them the same exposure and credibility as the major farm women's networks in the United States, Canada and Britain. The development of such a network is vital to the farm women in this study, and in Australia generally, if women are to win centrality, a communal focus and a political base.

Yet, while women are emerging from the shadows, this study shows that the process will be slow because women internalise their own subordinate position in society and undervalue their own efforts. A similar situation has been found by Ken Dempsey among the women in his Australian community study.[11] The marginalisation and undervaluing of women are aided by their lack of access to resources and to positions of authority within their communities. Dempsey's study points to the power of community censure in keeping women subordinate, and provides a persuasive explanation as to why women accept and internalise their inferior status. To challenge cultural norms and historical processes is to invite conflict within the family and censure within the community. The challenge to patriarchy must come not from individuals but from the community itself and from government instrumentalities.

THE FUTURE FOR WOMEN
IN AGRICULTURE

P redicting the future for women in agriculture is a difficult task and only informed speculations are possible. If governments continue to support technological advances in agriculture, then some farms will continue to expand and many farm families, unable to keep up with the trend, will be left behind in virtual poverty. Government analysts predict a leaner, tougher agriculture in the future, with a trend towards 'larger-than-family' farms accelerating. If such a scenario eventuates, then agriculture will continue to be 'defeminised' as women reduce their productive tasks and take on more off-farm work to generate income. However, the data from this study suggest there will considerable hardship in this future scenario. While some 'larger-than-family' farms were evident in this survey, a majority were family farms which had reduced their hired labour and were being operated by family members working long, hard hours. The tenacity of these families may be something that will obstruct the development of large-scale enterprises. Analysts need to consider carefully the consequences of a two-tiered system of agriculture, with larger farms at one end and smaller, poorer farms at the other.

What can be said, however, is that the patriarchal relations which dominate agriculture, and ideologies which support them, will ensure that women's future in agriculture will remain insignificant while ever such relations and ideologies go unchallenged. Women cannot become central players if each new generation of women are disinherited and obstructed from taking control of agricultural resources. Their entry into agriculture through marriage has made it difficult for them to have an equal role in agricultural production, because their own position may be ill defined and often, they are treated with suspicion by their husband's parents. The existence of inter- and intragenerational partnerships ensures that women have little or no legal status within the enterprise, while women who do gain legal status still find their position discounted in the wider community. Without community education to resist patriarchy and recognise the significant contribution that women make to family farming, women's position in agriculture will remain discounted and sub-ordinate. The evidence from this study demonstrates that younger women are losing their commitment to agriculture and to patri-lineal inheritance, and are, in many cases, encouraging their children to move away fromagriculture. This suggests that a crisis is looming. The lowering of the status of farming as an occupation in Australian society may see many more young male farmers unable to find women prepared to marry them and take on the burden of task performance expected of farm wives. Women's change in attitude may lead to a critical reduction in the numbers of family farmers within the next generation.

Yet, this study has demonstrated the enormous resilience of Australian farm women. As a researcher, I feel privileged to have met with so many farm women, and I am humbled by the open-ness with which I was made privy to the intimate details of their lives. My lasting impression of farm women is that they are tena-cious in defence of their family farming lifestyle, dedicated to the nurturance of their families, committed to ensuring viability for their farms and their industries and in tune with the land on which they live. Despite their public invisibility, the vast majority of women with whom I spoke evinced a great sense of self-worth and a contentment and satisfaction which comes from working closely with nature. I hope that this book achieves recognition and respect for the efforts of the many thousands of farm women in this country — past, present and future. Eliza Forlonge, whose contribution to agriculture was mentioned in Chapter 1 and whose name has been forgotten by all but a handful of scholars, is symbolic of the neglect of women's achievements and dedication to agriculture. It is now time to acknowledge the economic con-tributions of farm women and incorporate them into any analysis of agricultural production. If only for Eliza's sake!

NOTES

Chapter 1

1   ABS Catalogue no. 7102.0 Commonwealth Government Printer Canberra
2   Geoffrey Lawrence 1987 *Capitalism and the Countryside* Pluto Press: Sydney
3   Report on Deborah Peterson's address to Outlook Conference in Canberra in the *Sydney Morning Herald* 4 February 1994 p 1, and ABS 'Integrated Register Counts of Management Units by Agriculture and by Type of Legal Organisation' 1990
4   Kerry James 1989 *Women in Rural Australia* Queensland University Press: St Lucia p 2
5   Quoted in the *Wagga Wagga Daily Advertiser* 27 January 1989
6   Marilyn Lake 1987 *The Limits of Hope* Oxford University Press: Melbourne p 179
7   Census 1891 *Victorian Parliamentary Papers* 1893 vol 3 no 9:192
8   Marilyn Lake op. cit. pp 177–8.
9   For instance, Senator Bob Collins, Federal Minister for Primary Industry and Energy, acknowledged the vital role of women in agriculture during his address to delegates at the International Farm Women's Conference in Melbourne, July 1994. He vowed to work closely with Michael Lavarch, the Attorney General, to change the provisions of the Worker's Compensation Act which treat women on farms as 'sleeping partners'.
10   Michael Bittman 1991 *Juggling Time: How Australian Families Use Time* Office of the Status of Women, Department of the Prime Minister and Cabinet: Canberra
11   Margaret Alston 1993 'A Study of Australian Farm Women' unpublished PhD thesis, University of NSW
12   Caroline Sachs 1983 *The Invisible Farmers: Women in Agricultural Production* Rowan & Allanheld: Totawa, NJ p 49
13   ABS 1993 *Women in Australia* Canberra p 118
14   Sarah Whatmore 1991 *Farming Women: Gender, Work and Family Enterprise* Macmillan: London
15   Wava Haney 1983 'Farm Family and the Role of Women' in Gene F. Summers (ed.) *Technology and Social Change in Rural Areas* Westview Press: Boulder and London p 187
16   Elise Boulding 1980 'The Labour of United States Farm Women: A Knowledge Gap' *The Sociology of Work and Occupations* 7 (3) pp 261–90

17 Shirley Gould 1989 'Family Problems of Farm Women' in Kerry James (ed.) *Women in Rural Australia* University of Queensland Press: St Lucia pp 20–9
18 Alston op. cit.
19 Ken Dempsey 1992 *A Man's Town: Inequality Between Women and Men in Rural Australia* Oxford University Press: Melbourne
20 Alston op. cit.
21 Lawrence op. cit
22 ABARE *Farm Surveys Report* 1992 Canberra
23 Geoffrey Lawrence 1986 'Family Farming and Corporate Capitalism: The Uneasy Alliance' *Regional Journal of Social Issues* no. 18 December p 9

Chapter 2
1 Gretchen Poiner 1979 'Country Wives' *Australian and New Zealand Journal of Sociology* 15 (2) p 59
2 Hester Eisenstein 1984 *Contemporary Feminist Thought* Unwin Paperbacks: London and Sydney p 9
3 See, for instance, Jill Julius Matthews 1984 *Good and Mad Women* Allen & Unwin: Sydney
4 Zillah R. Eisenstein (ed.) 1979 *Capitalist Patriarchy and the Case for Socialist Feminism* Monthly Review Press: New York p 11
5 A. March 1982 'Female Invisibility in Androcentric Sociological Theory' *Insurgent Sociologist* 11 (2) p 100
6 Poiner op. cit. p 56
7 Frances Hill 1981 'Farm Women: Challenge to Scholarship' *Rural Sociologist.* 1 (6), p 370; Caroline E. Sachs 1983 *The Invisible Farmers: Women in Agricultural Production* Rowan & Allanheld: Totawa, NJ; Julie Williams 1992 *The Invisible Farmer: A Report on Australian Farm Women* Commonwealth Department of Primary Industries and Energy: Canberra
8 Ann Curthoys 1988 *For and Against Feminism* Allen & Unwin: Sydney p 11
9 Simone de Beauvoir 1984 *The Second Sex* Alfred A. Knopf: New York, p 16
10 Hester Eisenstein op. cit. p xii
11 Jo Little 1986 'Feminist Perspectives in Rural Geography: An Introduction' *Journal of Rural Studies* 2 p 2
12 Kate Millet 1970 *Sexual Politics* Avon Books: New York
13 Hester Eisenstein op. cit. p 7
14 For an in-depth discussion of the concept of wifehood, see Sarah Whatmore 1991 *Farming Women: Gender Work and Family Enterprise* Macmillan: London
15 Poiner op. cit. p 24
16 S. Stebbings 1984 'Women in the Countryside: A Study of Women's Role Perceptions in Two Kent Parishes' in T. Bradley and P. Lowe *Locality and Rurality: Economy and Society in Rural Regions* Geo Books: Norwich p 202
17 J. Bell and U. Pandey 1989 The Exclusion of Women from Australian Post-Secondary Agricultural Education, 1880–1970, University of New England, Armidale
18 See Ken Dempsey 1992 *A Man's Town: Inequality Between Women and Men in Rural Australia* Oxford University Press: Melbourne for a discussion of the sanctions imposed on women who challenge the established order.
19 Tracy Bachrach Ehlers 1987 'The Matrifocal Farm' in M. Chibrik (ed.) *Farm Work and Fieldwork: American Agriculture in Anthropological Perspective* Ithaca, NY p 146
20 Curthoys op. cit. p 59

Notes

21 Notably, Geoffrey Lawrence 1987 *Capitalism and the Countryside* Pluto Press: Sydney; and Wava Haney 1983 'Farm Family and the Role of Women' in Gene F. Summers (ed.) *Technology and Social Change in Rural Areas* Westview Press: Boulder and London

22 Curthoys op. cit. p 22

23 Millet op. cit.

24 Curthoys op. cit. p 85

25 Little op. cit. p 2

26 Clare Burton 1983 *Subordination: Feminisism and Social Theory* Allen & Unwin Sydney p xiii

27 Curthoys op. cit. p 91

28 Ruth Gasson 1979 'The Role of the Farmer's Wife in Australia' in conference proceedings *The Woman in Country Australia Looks Ahead* McMillan Rural Studies Centre: Warragul

29 Catherine Chan 1983 *Divorce: An Australian Women's Guide* William Heinemann: Australia

30 Ingolf Vogeler 1981 *The Myth of the Family Farm: Agribusiness Dominance of US Agriculture* Westview Press: Boulder Col

31 Lyla Coorey 1989 Domestic Violence and the Police: Who Is Being Protected? A Rural Australian View unpublished Masters thesis, Department of Social Work and Social Policy, University of Sydney

32 See, for instance, Millet op. cit.; Elizabeth Janeway 1971 *Man's World, Women's Place: A Study in Social Mythology* Dell Publishing: New York; Dorothy Dinnerstein 1977 *The Mermaid and the Minotaur: Sexual Arrangements and Human Malaise.* Harper & Row: New York; Zillah Eisenstein op. cit. and Little op. cit.

33 Little op. cit. p 2

34 Hester Eisenstein op. cit. p xi

35 ibid. p xii

36 ibid. p xii

37 See, for instance, Nancy Chodorow 1979 'Mothering, Male Dominance and Capitalism' in Zillah Eisenstein op. cit. p 83 and Dinnerstein op. cit. p 10

38 Shulamith Firestone 1970 *The Dialectic of Sex: The Case for Feminist Revolution* Bantam Books: New York, p 2

39 See, for instance Juliet Mitchell 1971 *Woman's Estate* Vintage Books: New York, p 87 and Zillah Eisenstein op. cit. p 19

40 Janeway op. cit. p 11

41 Millet op. cit. p 24

42 Zillah Eisenstein op. cit. p 92

43 Chodorow op. cit. p 92 and Sachs op. cit. p 69

44 See, for instance, Janeway op. cit. and Mitchell op. cit.

45 See, for example, Firestone op. cit.; Sherry Ortner 1974 'Is Female to Male as Nature is to Culture?' in M. Z. Rosaldo and L. Lamphere (eds) *Women, Culture and Society* Stanford University Press: Stanford; Michelle Zimbalist Rosaldo 1974 'Women, Culture and Society: A Theoretical Overview' in Rosaldo and Lamphere op. cit.

46 See Janeway op. cit., Millet op. cit. and Firestone op. cit.

47 Gretchen Poiner 1990 *The Good Old Rule: Gender and Other Power Relationships in a Rural Community* Sydney University Press: Sydney

48 See Ann Oakley 1985 *The Sociology of Housework* Basil Blackwell Inc.: London for a discussion of the concept of 'private power'

49 Seena Kohl 1977 'Women's Participation in the North American Family Farm'

Notes

Women's Studies International Quarterly 1 p 13

50 Janeway op. cit. p 56
51 Miriam Dixson 1984 *The Real Matilda* Penguin: Ringwood p 16
52 See, for instance, Janeen Baxter, Diane Gibson, Coralie Kingston and John Western 1988 *The Lives of Rural Women: Problems and Prospects of Employment* Department of Anthropology and Sociology University of Queensland p 16 and Rachel Ann Rosenfeld 1985 *Farm Women: Work, Farm and Family in the United States* University of North Carolina Press: Chapel Hill
53 Gould Colman and Sarah Elbert 1984 'Farming Families: The Farm Needs Everyone' *Research in Rural Sociology and Development* 1 p 66
54 Sarah Elbert 1988 'Women and Farming: Changing Structures, Changing Roles' in Haney and Knowles (eds) *Women and Farming: Changing Roles, Changing Structures* Westview Press: Boulder and London p 263

Chapter 3
1 Marilyn Lake 1987 *The Limits of Hope* Oxford University Press: Melbourne
2 Deborah Fink 1986 *Open Country Iowa: Rural Women, Tradition and Change* State University of New York Press: Albany
3 Lake op. cit. p 188
4 Ann Moylan 1989 *Women and the Telephone in Australia: A Study Prepared for Telecom Australia* Telecom: Australia
5 Fink op. cit.
6 ibid.
7 ibid.
8 Sarah Whatmore 1991 *Farming Women: Gender, Work and Family Enterprise* Macmillan: London
9 Julian Cribb 1982 *The Forgotten Country* Australasian Farm Publications: Melbourne p 7
10 Geoffrey Lawrence 1987 *Capitalism and the Countryside.* Pluto Press: Sydney
11 Lawrence op. cit. p 159
12 See Geoffrey Lawrence 1986 'Class in Australian Rural Society' *Occasional Papers in Community Studies* 5/86 Phillip Institute of Technology: Coburg, Vic. and Brian Furze 1987 'Capitalist Agriculture and the Need for an Ecologically Sound Alternative' *Regional Journal of Social Issues* 20 pp 37–8
13 Susan A. Mann and James M. Dickinson 1978 'Obstacles to the Development of a Capitalist Agriculture' *The Journal of Peasant Studies* 5 p 471
14 David Goodman, Bernardo Sorj and John Wilkinson 1987 *From Farming to Biotechnology* Basil Blackwell: London
15 Rachel Rosenfeld 1985 op. cit. p 23

Chapter 4
1 Frances Hill 1981 'Farm Women: Challenge to Scholarship' *Rural Sociologist* 1 (6) p 373
2 Sarah Elbert 1981 'The Challenge of Research on Farm Women' *Rural Sociologist* 1 (6), p 387
3 ABARE *Farm Surveys Report* Canberra 1993
4 See Caroline E. Sachs 1983 *The Invisible Farmers: Women in Agricultural Production* Rowan & Allanheld: Totawa NJ p 81 and Jessica Pearson 1979 'Note on Female Farmers' *Rural Sociology* 44 (1) p 199
5 Sachs op. cit. p 82 and Tracy Bachrach Ehlers 1987 'The Matrifocal Farm' in M. Chibrik (ed.) *Farm work and Fieldwork: American Agriculture in Anthropological*

Perspective Ithaca: NY p 146
6   Ehlers op. cit. p 152
7   Sarah Whatmore 1991 *Farming Women: Gender, Work and Family Enterprise* Macmillan: London p 99

Chapter 5
1   See, for example, Elizabeth Janeway 1971 *Man's World, Women's Place: A Study in Social Mythology* Dell Publishing: New York and Ann Oakley 1985 *The Sociology of Housework* Basil Blackwell Inc.: London
2   Margaret Alston 1993 'A Study of Australian Farm Women' unpublished PhD thesis, University of NSW
3   Wava G. Haney and Jane B. Knowles 1988 *Women and Farming: Changing Roles, Changing Structures* Westview Press: Boulder and London
4   Gretchen Poiner 1990 *The Good Old Rule: Gender and Other Power Relationships in a Rural Community* Sydney University Press: Sydney pp 137–8
5   See, for example, Ian Gray 1991 *Politics in Place* Cambridge University Press: Sydney and Gillian Cowlishaw 1988 *Black, White or Brindle: Race in Rural Australia* Cambridge University Press: Sydney.
6   Poiner op. cit.

Chapter 6
1   Ken Dempsey 1990 *Smalltown: A Study of Rural Inequality, Cohesion and Belonging* Oxford University Press: Melbourne
2   Elise Boulding 1980 'The Labour of United States Farm Women: A Knowledge Gap' *Sociology of Work and Occupations* 7 (3) p 283
3   Sarah Whatmore 1991 *Farming Women: Gender, Work and Family Enterprise* Macmillan: London pp 93–4
4   Whatmore op. cit. p 103

Chapter 7
1   See, for example, Seena B. Kohl 1977 'Women's Participation in the North American Family Farm' *Women's Studies International Quarterly* 1 pp 47–54 and Ruth Gasson 1984 'Farm Women in Europe: Their Need for Off-Farm Employment'. *Sociologia Ruralis* xxiv pp 216–27

Chapter 8
1   William P. Heffernan, G. Green, P. Lesley and M. Nolan 1981 'Part Time Farming and the Rural Community' *Rural Sociology* 46 (summer) p 245

Chapter 9
1   Margaret Alston 1993 'A Study of Australian Farm Women' unpublished PhD thesis, University of NSW.
2   Sarah Elbert 1988 'Women and Farming: Changing Structures, Changing Roles' in Haney and Knowles (eds) *Women and Farming: Changing Roles, Changing Structures* Westview Press: Boulder and London p 248
3   Geoffrey Lawrence 1986 'Family Farming and Corporate Capitalism: The Uneasy Alliance' *Regional Journal of Social Issues* 18 (December)
4   Margaret Alston 1992 'Editorial: Rural Australia' *Australian Social Work* (June)

Chapter 10
1   Sarah Whatmore 1991 *Farming Women: Gender, Work and Family Enterprise* Macmillan: London

Chapter 11

1   Ruth Gasson 1992 'Farmer's Wives: Their Contribution to the Farm Business' *Journal of Agricultural Economics* 43 1 (January) p 84

2   Richard Le Heron, Mike Roche, Tom Johnston and Susan Bowler 1990 'Pluriactivity in NZ's Agro-Commodity Chains' paper presented to the NZ Sociological Association Conference, Lincoln University: Canterbury

3   Gasson op. cit. p 85

4   Sally Shortall 1990 'Power Analysis and Farm Wives: An Empirical Study of the Power Relations Affecting Women on Irish Farms' Dept of Sociology, McGill University: Canada

5   Gretchen Poiner 1990 *The Good Old Rule: Gender and Other Power Relationships in a Rural Community* Sydney University Press: Sydney p 184

6   Shortall op. cit.

7   Sarah Whatmore 1991 *Farming Women: Gender Work and Family* Macmillan: London p 35

8   Cornelia Butler Flora and Sue Johnson 1978 'Discarding the Distaff: New Roles for Rural Women' in Thomas Ford (ed.) *Rural USA Persistence and Change* Iowa University Press: Ames; and Gasson op. cit.

9   Deborah Fink 1986 *Open Country Iowa: Rural Women, Tradition and Change* State University of New York Press: Albany

10 Frances M. Shaver 1988 'Women Work and Transformations in Agricultural Production' paper presented to World Congress of Rural Sociology, Bologna, Italy, and Max J. Pfeffer 1989 'The Feminisation of Production on Part-time Farms in the Federal Republic of Germany' *Rural Sociology* 54 (1) pp 60–73

11 Ken Dempsey 1992 *A Man's Town: Inequality Between Women and Men in Rural Australia* University of Queensland Press: St Lucia

INDEX